Carol Mullens

Linda Nielsen

How to motivate adolescents

A GUIDE FOR PARENTS, TEACHERS, AND COUNSELORS

A SPECTRUM BOOK

Prentice-Hall, Inc., Englewood Cliffs, New Jersey 07632

Library of Congress Cataloging in Publication Data

Nielsen, Linda.
    How to motivate adolescents.

    "A Spectrum Book."
    Includes bibliographical references and index.
    1. Adolescence.   2. Adolescent psychology—United
States.   3. Motivation (Psychology).   4. Sex role—
United States.   5. Minority youth—United States.
I. Title.
HQ796.N545 1982   305.2'35   82-9090
ISBN 0-13-424010-3   AACR2
ISBN 0-13-424002-2 (pbk.)

The picture on page 133 is from *Hope and Dignity: Older Black Women of North Carolina* by Susan Mullally. © 1981 by Susan Mullally. It is used by permission of the author. The photographs on pages 103 and 137 are used by permission of Winston-Salem-Forsyth County School System.

1 2 3 4 5 6 7 8 9 10

ISBN 0-13-424010-3

ISBN 0-13-424002-2 {PBK.}

Editorial/production supervision by Maxine Bartow
Cover design by Jeannette Jacobs
Manufacturing buyer: Cathie Lenard

Prentice-Hall International, Inc., *London*
Prentice-Hall of Australia Pty. Limited, *Sydney*
Prentice-Hall Canada Inc., *Toronto*
Prentice-Hall of India Private Limited, *New Delhi*
Prentice-Hall of Japan, Inc., *Tokyo*
Prentice-Hall of Southeast Asia Pte. Ltd., *Singapore*
Whitehall Books Limited, *Wellington, New Zealand*

For Alan, who encouraged me unselfishly
and who lived the year with dignity and courage,
and for Bear, who warded off pain and pettiness
with his love and laughter.

Contents

THE IMPACT OF PHYSICAL NEEDS AND SEX ROLES ON MOTIVATION

SPECIAL MOTIVATIONAL PROBLEMS

THE INFLUENCE OF FAMILY AND FRIENDS ON MOTIVATION

Preface

How was I to react when Joe Romines called me "an old lop-eared heifer" because he was so frustrated practicing the short vowel sounds? What was I to do with sixteen year olds who read at a fourth-grade level and thought that "far" was what caused buildings to burn; What was I to say to the angry young man with cerebral palsy who told me to go to hell in front of the whole class? And what had I done right when Troy, a delinquent, still carried in his wallet a complimentary note that I had written his parents four years earlier? Believing that love and empathy were essentially what adolescents needed, I spent endless hours listening to their woeful tales. I also felt guilty about the economic advantages I had grown up with and the society I profited from. But my guilt and pity taught few kids to read better or to stay out of trouble. When we did advance, it was not love that got us there, but the specific methods of motivating adolescents that I stumbled on by trial and error over the years. For the sake of all the Troys and Joe Romines, I wish I had those years back again to help them as I now feel more equipped to do.

The thesis of this book is that motivation is not an alien being that resides inside some adolescents and deserts others. Whether or not adolescents are motivated to achieve academically or to behave appropriately depends mainly on the way we structure their environment and interact with them. Some adults seem to know the techniques almost instinctively, but the rest of us have to work diligently and systematically to learn specific methods for motivating adolescents.

Unfortunately, most books about adolescence do not offer advice for motivating or assisting youngsters. A lot of textbook information is of the "so what?" variety. "So what" difference does it make if you know the average age of menarche when one student is lighting a match to the trashcan and when none of them can read? In this text I have tried to integrate practical ideas from several disciplines. The suggestions are intended for teachers, psychiatric workers, counselors, principals, social workers, and students preparing for these vocations. Parents and adolescents can also profit from many of the chapters. I do not want to reinforce the image that most adolescents are unmotivated or troubled. Indeed, the majority are not. But almost all adolescents (and adults!) occasionally feel that their "get-up-and-go" has got up and went. This book is designed to help youngsters through those troubled times, not to tackle such severe problems as drug addiction or suicidal depression.

Each of the book's four sections considers aspects of adolescent motivation that are seldom mentioned in other texts. Part One describes ways in which schools undermine or create adolescent motivation. These chapters show how schools can enhance academic motivation and improve conduct without resorting to corporal punishment or suspensions. Although many books describe physiological changes during adolescence and sex role stereotypes, few help us see the practical applications of this information. Part Two does so by suggesting ways to use data about physiology and sex roles to motivate adolescents who have not fulfilled their potential. Part Three recommends specific ways to assist youth from minority cultures and youngsters with special motivational problems. Rather than devoting a few paragraphs to global platitudes about treating minorities fairly, Chapter 7 summarizes many specific recommendations for helping black, Hispanic, Asian, and Indian youth. Part Four explains how friends and families can affect an adolescent's motivation, emphasizing the positive aspects of the peer group and offering procedures for motivating adolescents by teaching them self-management skills.

Throughout every chapter I have tried to maintain perspectives that are not racist, sexist, or ethnocentric. I have also included specific suggestions for motivating adolescents who are usually ignored in other books, such as athletes, rural Americans, the physically handicapped, adolescent girls, bilingual youngsters, the gifted, and the learning disabled. The book's recommendations are based on research that is both recent and scholarly.

Although I would like to have offered detailed instructions for implementing the techniques mentioned in each chapter, space was too limited for that endeavor. My goal has been to tempt readers to experiment with new procedures and to read the contemporary books cited in my footnotes. Without wanting to be accused of advocating a haphazard approach to motivation, I have offered a variety of techniques rather than patronizing one theoretical viewpoint. (Both sides of every theoretical argument will claim to have God and logic on their side.) But adults who work with adolescents know that no single approach is appropriate for motivating every youngster.

My few intimate friends are precious sources of energy that indirectly underlie all my writing. I appreciate them and the individuals who made specific contributions to this text. For her patience in forwarding mail, books, supplies, and nurturance, I thank Betty Veach. A besieged provost, Ed Wilson, generously squeezed more water from the stone and found money for the typing of my manuscript. Anne Mathews has earned every right to feel proud of herself for typing many poorly penned pages of this work. And Helen Hyams meticulously edited and enhanced the quality of each chapter.

But without financial support from the American Association of University Women, I would not have had the most essential ingredient for my writing—time. Not believing I had really received the postdoctoral fellowship, I telephoned twice to be sure I had heard correctly when the voice announced, "Yes, you won." For their willingness to make a financial investment in a young writer and for their commitment to women, I am profoundly grateful to the American Association of University Women.

Winner of the 1980 author's award from the U.S. Center for Women Scholars, **Linda Nielsen** has directed many workshops for teachers and has served as a research director of several federal programs for adolescents. Dr. Nielsen has written numerous articles and one book based on her experiences as a public school teacher and her research with delinquents and underachievers. A university teacher since 1974, Dr. Nielsen has a degree in counseling and a doctorate in educational psychology.

part one

THE SCHOOL'S ROLE IN MOTIVATION

chapter one

Understanding underachievement

UNDERACHIEVEMENT'S TOLL ON SOCIETY

Why should taxpayers worry about the academic achievement of other people's children? As long as a family's own adolescents are succeeding at school and in the community, why despair over someone else's problems? Casually spoken words such as empathy, civil rights, or justice might be reason enough for some adults to be concerned about all adolescents' underachievement. But some educators go so far as to say that the major obstacle to eliminating illiteracy is the apathy of literate folks who do not see illiteracy as any threat to their own well-being.[1] Two convincing reasons for caring about America's adolescents are money and safety.

Adolescents whose academic problems are unresolved are the most likely to drop out of school, commit delinquent acts, vandalize property in the community, marry young, become teenaged parents, and develop into adult criminals.[2] For taxpayers, these situations eventually mean payments for aid to dependent children, incarcerating delinquents and adult criminals, social services for the unemployed, and reparations for damaged property. Sending an adolescent to college for four years costs approximately twenty thousand dollars, and comparable time for an imprisoned youth costs taxpayers about fifty thousand dollars.[3] In 1978 over 650,000 students between fourteen and seventeen years old were at least one year behind their grade level. If better education had prevented these academic failures, taxpayers could have saved the 1.3 billion dollars that was used to send these youngsters back through the same grade again.[4] Consumer prices are also related to academic underachievement. In 1972 the Bell Telephone Company alone spent twenty-five million dollars on basic education programs for employees.[5] Consumers helped defray these costs in their phone bills.

Every adolescent with academic problems is certainly not a delinquent or a burden to society. But almost every troubled adolescent is failing or struggling academically. Studies repeatedly show that poorly behaved youths and delinquents are plagued by learning disabilities, repeated failure at school, reading and math deficits, and hearing or speech disorders.[6] Correcting adolescents' academic problems usually eliminates their destructive conduct.

Unfortunately, adults often invest more time in devising clever schemes to control misbehavior than in teaching academic skills. This is especially true when students are not white, middle-class children.[7] A vicious cycle grows: Adults invest time worrying about discipline while students misbehave in reaction to their academic frustration. An adolescent who spends forty hours a week feeling frustrated and inadequate at school is a prime candidate for aggressive, delinquent, or self-destructive acts. Although we do not usually have any power to alter an adolescent's family or personal history, we could wage a mighty battle against academic underachievement in America's secondary schools. Will we?

DEFINITIONS OF UNDERACHIEVEMENT

The boy was not fluent in his native language at the age of nine. He barely graduated from high school, attended a polytechnic institute instead of college, and worked in a patent office because his academic record was too weak to secure him a better job. In his mid-twenties this young man was revolutionizing the science of physics. Was the boy an adolescent underachiever? Yes, Einstein was: "My intellectual development was retarded, as a result of which I began to wonder about space and time only when I had already grown up."[8]

What is an underachiever? One way of defining underachievement is to compare an individual's performance to the national averages for people of the same age. Fifteen year olds who read at a fourth-grade level, therefore, are underachievers if most Americans of that age read at a tenth-grade level. Students who cannot muster the energy for one sit-up are also underachievers by national standards. But relying exclusively on national or local averages to distinguish motivated from unmotivated adolescents creates two dilemmas. First, we may fail to help youngsters reach their potential if they score adequately on achievement tests. Second, we may prod or criticize adolescents whose skills are below national standards but who are using all of their potential in very motivated ways. Suppose, for instance, that slim, muscular Agatha, who could run five miles with minimal training, always chooses to amble off the track after one mile, still surpassing the national average for girls her age. Now assume that fat Albert practices religiously until he is finally able to run two laps, which is still far below his peer group's average. Most of us probably would not accuse Albert of being lazy or consult a specialist to help us motivate him. But many of us would chastise Agatha and try to make her "fulfill her potential." But what if we should then discover that Agatha has been suffering from mononucleosis? What if we should further discover in the latest medical journal that overweight people have an advantage over their skinnier peers in running? Now who is the overachiever and who is the underachiever?

We respond to adolescents on the basis of what we believe their mental or physical limits are. An underachiever is someone who might benefit from our assistance to use his or her mental or physical talents more effectively. National averages may show where students' performances rank in comparison to most people their age, but the scores do not define any individual's actual limits. Deciding who is motivated means predicting individuals' capabilities. If we underestimate an adolescent's physical or mental abilities, we might accept performance that never taps his or her talents. Believing they have reached their limits, we may not try to motivate certain youngsters who could profit from our help. On the other hand, overestimating someone's capacities creates needless stress and unfair recrimination. Unfortunately, even the best estimations of a person's limits can be embarrassingly wrong, as Einstein demonstrates.

At present we do not have instruments reliable enough to peek inside an adolescent, measure physical and intellectual potential, and stick a label on the owner: "high potential," "low potential," "no potential." Because defining underachievement is so difficult, our wisest strategy is to try to motivate all adolescents to expand their skills without punishing failure.

THE EXTENT OF UNDERACHIEVEMENT

Although identifying adolescents who are not using their potential is difficult, one clue is to compare the academic skills of various groups on national achievement tests (Table 1). Although some improvements in mathematical skills have occurred since 1973, black, urban, western, and southeastern students were still below national norms for math performance in 1979. Until the age of seventeen, girls perform as well as boys mathematically. Disadvantaged urban students show the greatest declines in math, and blacks seem to lose their mathematical gains by age seventeen. The national assessment committee concludes that the "back to basics" movement, with its emphasis on rote memorization and drill, has narrowed the curriculum so that students are deprived of practice in solving the more complex mathematical problems.[9]

National results in reading skills are similar to those in mathematics.[10] Between 1970 and 1980 adolescents' abilities in literal comprehension, spelling, and punctuation remained virtually unchanged, but the quality and coherence of writing for thirteen and seventeen year olds declined. Seventeen year olds performed more poorly in 1980 than in 1970 on tests requiring them to comprehend written materials by inferring the meaning. Blacks, boys, and southeastern students came closer to the national reading averages in 1980 but were still less skilled than girls and wealthy white youngsters. A surprising result is that the most talented seventeen year olds in 1980 were reading more poorly than gifted students in 1970. Apparently many bright students need help motivating themselves to fulfill more of their potential in reading skills.

The academic skills of minority youth and girls are even more disturbing. In some ways progress has occurred quickly for blacks, Indians, and Hispanics. In 1940, 41 percent of white Americans completed twelve years of school compared to 12 percent of minorities. By 1979 87 percent of whites finished twelve years of school compared to 76 percent of minorities.[11] In 1980, 95 percent of all adolescents were enrolled in school and three-fourths of these students graduated.[12] But underachievement remains a serious issue for minorities. Dropout rates in 1979 were approximately 50 percent for Mexican-Americans, 65 percent for Puerto Ricans, 45 percent for Indians, 80 percent for children of migrant workers, 50 percent for blacks, and 25 percent for Caucasions.[13] Thousands of Indian and Hispanic adolescents whose native language is not English are also educationally handicapped in American schools.[14]

THE EFFECTIVENESS
OF SECONDARY EDUCATION

Some critics argue that public schools cannot significantly improve adolescent achievement. In 1979, 15,335,000 youngsters were enrolled in grades nine through twelve, with 13,740,000 of them in public schools and 10,000 in schools run by the Bureau of Indian Affairs.[15] Minority students' enrollment in private schools rose 20 percent from 1978 to 1980; almost a third of the children in private schools came from homes with incomes of less than fifteen thousand dollars a year.[16] The federal government is even considering tax credits for parents who want to send their children to private schools. Clearly there is concern that investing money in public education is wasteful and unproductive.

One view of public education is that correcting society's economic inequities is the only way to significantly improve educational and vocational achievement.[17] Since the qualitative differences among schools appear to have no profound or long-term effect on students, the solution to underachievement is not to improve schools but to reduce the huge discrepancies between rich and poor Americans' incomes.

Another negative judgment of public schools is that only private education can reduce underachievement and disciplinary problems.[18] Private schools are supposedly more orderly, safer, and more disciplined than public schools. By requiring more homework and more courses in math, science, and English, they create more productive students.

Coleman's first report in 1966 also criticized public schools, claiming that the quality of a school had relatively little impact on youngsters. Although the 1981 Coleman Report criticized public education and endorsed a voucher system to support private schools, the encouraging conclusion is that schools can indeed make a significant difference in a child's academic

TABLE 1. National Assessment of Educational Progress for Seventeen Year Olds

Selected characteristics of participants	Career and occupational development	Reading	Art	Citizenship	Social studies	Science	Math
National average: percentage of correct answers	72.8	72.0	53.0	67.4	67.6	53.5	59.0
Percentage difference from national norm:							
Northeast	0.4	1.5	1.1	0.8	0.8	2.2	3.5
Southeast	-2.9	-4.1	-3.1	-2.2	-2.4	-4.1	-4.6
Central	1.7	2.4	1.1	0.9	0.9	1.2	2.6
West	-0.3	-1.0	0.2	0.1	0.2	-0.8	-2.8
Male	-0.4	-1.9	-1.3	0.0	0.2	2.6	2.6
Female	0.4	1.8	1.3	0.0	-0.2	-2.5	-2.5
Black	-12.1	-16.6	-7.7	-8.6	-9.4	-15.7	-17.8
White	1.8	2.8	1.4	1.6	1.6	2.6	3.0

Parental education:							
No high school	−7.1	−10.3	−7.4	−6.4	−6.6	−8.0	−10.8
Some high school	−4.7	−6.9	−4.8				
Graduated high school	−0.9	−1.2	−1.4	−1.5	−1.5	−1.8	−3.0
Post-high school	3.4	5.1	4.4	4.6	4.6	5.1	6.2
Size and type of community:							
Low metropolitan	−6.4	−9.2	−2.7	−5.8	−6.1	−12.3	−12.8
Extreme rural	0.2	−1.7	−2.8	−0.1	−0.3	0.0	−2.2
Small place	0.2	0.6	−0.7	0.2	0.2	0.6	−1.5
Medium city	0.6	0.0	−0.2	0.2	−0.2	1.7	3.6
Main big city	0.4	−0.1	0.7	−1.2	−1.2	−2.6	−2.4
Urban fringe	0.9	2.2	1.8	0.8	0.8	2.4	3.8
High metropolitan	3.4	6.7	4.6	4.2	4.2	4.4	9.9

Note: Data are for the following years: 1973-74: Career and occupational development; 1974-75: Reading, Art; 1975-76: Citizenship, social studies; 1976-77: Science; 1977-78: Math.

Source: Taken from material available in the files of National Assessment of Educational Progress, Denver, Colorado, December 1978.

performance. Despite a child's family background or income, Coleman claims that a school has the power to create academically and socially skilled students.

The most heartening research conclusion is that public schools most certainly can, and do, improve adolescents' academic skills. A study of twelve inner-city schools in London showed that teachers' styles and the curriculum affect adolescents' academic achievement and conduct.[19] Students who attended schools were adults praised them and provided a carefully planned curriculum succeeded academically. Adolescents with similar personalities and family backgrounds, however, underachieved and misbehaved in schools which used punishment, competitive grading, failure, and authoritarian methods to control students. American researchers have also agreed that teachers can make a profound impact on the academic and social skills of adolescents, despite differences among families.[20]

Undeniably secondary schools are still unable to remedy the academic problems of many American youth. But research at present does not indicate that investing money in public education is like pouring money into a leaky bucket.

ADOLESCENTS' AND TEACHERS' ATTITUDES TOWARD SCHOOL

Most secondary school teachers are seeking advice about motivating apathetic youth and managing disruptive ones. Talented adults who work with the unmotivated and undisciplined, despite their affection for adolescents, "burn out" quickly and often leave the profession after several years. Many faculty members are discouraged by large classes, lack of parental involvement, inadequate materials, and insufficient remedial programs in high schools. More dissatisfied than elementary teachers, high school faculties often feel that students do not value an education.[21]

Most adolescents feel that school is just "okay," not an excruciating or exhilarating experience.[22] The youngsters with the fewest academic skills are usually unhappy and convinced that their teachers dislike them. Yet even many college students who succeeded in high school cite an incident in school when asked to recall their most negative experience in life. In a 1972 national study, almost half of the high school seniors surveyed blamed underachievement on their own study habits.[23] But 90 percent of these students were dissatisfied with the amount of help they received in math and reading from their teachers. Many felt that their teachers were not interested in them, and 80 percent said that lecturing was still the most popular instructional method. Most adolescents say that their school's primary values are competition, obedience, and achievement.[24] Students whose personal values differ from the school's are the least satisfied with education. Although feelings about school usually depend on an individual's classroom success, academic difficulties still account for more referrals of adolescents for professional counseling than any other problem.[25]

SELF-CONCEPT AND UNDERACHIEVEMENT

Some advisors say that improving an adolescent's self-concept is the solution to academic and behavioral problems. Many adults are consequently told to accept everyone with "unconditional positive regard." Although this advice may seem very humanistic, research has not shown that enhancing self-esteem benefits most youngsters academically or behaviorally.[26] In fact some children from low-income homes who perform poorly in school have higher self-concept scores than their rich, successful classmates.[27] Most adolescents' self-esteem fluctuates, depending on the feedback others send them about their skills in a particular situation.

Adolescents generally establish self-confidence and self-satisfaction as a consequence of success at school. Low self-concept scores often result from repeated academic, social, or physical failure. But self-esteem is *not* a prerequisite for academic, athletic, or social achievement; it is the *consequence* of success. We are doing youngsters a grave injustice by blaming their underachievement on a poor self-concept or by merely assuring them that they are unconditionally loved and accepted. The humane gesture is to teach youngsters specific ways to master the physical, academic, or social skills that create self-esteem.

INTELLIGENCE TESTS AND UNDERACHIEVEMENT

In addition to tests for self-concept, many people still rely on intelligence test scores to explain adolescents' academic achievement and conduct. But what does an intelligence test actually measure? How should a score influence adults who work with adolescents? How fair and valid are the tests? Does intelligence testing do more harm than good?

The tests' proponents believe the scores are accurate, reliable measures of an individual's intellectual potential. A student with a score of 85 is, therefore, incapable of learning the same concepts or skills as someone with a score of 120. One of the most famous defenders of intelligence tests, Arthur Jensen, claims that 80 percent of the score is due to inherited abilities that experience cannot alter. Jensen's most controversial assertion is that some races have superior abilities as a consequence of unalterable genetic endowments. He bases his conclusions on intelligence test scores from World War II servicemen and subsequent research in which the average score of black Americans is lower than the scores of other races even when financial status and recent immigration is considered. Chinese-Americans scored highest, then Caucasions, Indians and blacks. Jensen contends that the tests are not culturally biased because blacks and Caucasions usually miss the same difficult questions. The test scores are also correlated with most students' grades in school.

Jensen cites studies in which identical twins raised in different environments will have virtually the same intelligence scores. Dutch children who were malnourished during World War II also had scores similar to those of the well-fed children of their race. Jensen believes that compensatory education projects such as Project Head Start fail to improve achievement because cognitive differences are genetic, not environmental. Defending himself against the inevitable charges of racism, Jensen said, "None of my research lets you conclude anything about the intelligence of any individual black or white person."[28] Because the research uses "averaged" scores from each race, a prediction about a single person's intelligence on the basis of skin color would be invalid. Jensen implores liberals and humanitarians to accept his conclusions and to relinquish the sentimental, naive myth that all races are intellectually equal at birth. President Nixon, who vetoed legislation for child care programs, and politicians who later slashed compensatory education funds were influenced by Jensen's theories. These politicians considered the expenditures for compensatory programs wasteful, since intelligence was presumed to be genetically determined.

Jensen's opponents argue that an intelligence test primarily measures what an individual has learned from a white, middle class culture.[29] The tests measure acquired knowledge, but not intellectual potential. Intelligence tests ask questions on math, definitions of words, historical and scientific facts, and moral dilemmas that supposedly have "correct" answers—those of the white middle class. For example, students are asked who discovered America and what they should do if someone hits them. A Native American may consider the first question biased. The answers that are considered "correct" for the second question clearly represent upper-middle-class values: Tell an adult, discuss the problem with the attacker, or walk away. Some critics of the test believe the questions should represent each student's own culture.

Robert Williams, designer of the "Bitch Test" (Black Intelligence Test of Cultural Homogeneity), condemns intelligence testing as "scientific racism" that underwrites racial discrimination.[30] Like Williams, other opponents of intelligence tests believe low scores often result from a poor education, nutritional deficits, weak test-taking skills, inadequate parenting, and culturally biased questions.

What data support the critics of intelligence tests?[31] First, studies involving thousands of children show that compensatory education can raise intelligence test scores by as much as ten points. This often means the distinction between "retarded" and "average," or "average" and "gifted." The greatest improvements occur when parents are trained to stimulate infants at home. Other programs, which teach parenting skills to retarded mothers in combination with child-care centers, have increased some children's test scores by thirty points. These researchers believe that parenting skills have enough impact on a child's intelligence to warrant high school courses that teach adolescents how to be effective parents. In other studies, black children adopted by white professionals eventually scored higher on IQ tests than did their peers in less wealthy homes. Birth order also seems to affect intelligence scores, with the firstborn child scoring higher than other siblings; this may be due to the extra attention and mental stimulation the child receives from its parents before siblings come along. Some researchers even raise students' scores by teaching them test-taking skills: reading directions carefully, using the deductive method, and talking softly to themselves while solving problems.[32]

In 1976 the American Psychological Association postponed a resolution that all psychological tests include a warning about their potentially harmful consequences on students who differed from the people on whom the test was standardized.[33] The APA merely recommended that abuses in testing are to be avoided. But in 1979 a California judge ruled that intelligence tests were racially biased and must be discontinued as the means for placing students into special classes.[34] A pending decision by the Supreme Court could result in a nationwide ban.

Amid all the turmoil, two certainties remain. First, psychologists do not agree that any test accurately or fairly assesses intellectual potential. Second, an erroneous judgment about intelligence can have devastating effects on a person's life. Many reliable, noncontroversial instruments exist for identifying a student's academic problems, such as tests for learning disabilities and reading or math skills. The information from these tests can help in designing a curriculum and teaching strategy that will combat a student's specific deficits. With these diagnostic tools, testing for "intelligence" seems superfluous and hazardous.

THEORIES OF MOTIVATION

If intelligence and self-concept tests are not very reliable explanations for underachievement, what is? Can anyone explain why some youngsters are more motivated academically and more well-behaved than others? Psychologists have been studying human motivation for decades. But each theory has shortcomings and contradictions that render a complete understanding of motivation impossible, although each has some indirect application to adolescents and is worth a brief review.[35]

Psychoanalytic Theory

Sigmund Freud's psychoanalytic theory dominated psychology from 1900 until the 1930s. Freud believed that people are motivated by innate drives, primarily sex and aggression. A person's conduct is always aimed at fulfilling sexual and aggressive needs, thereby reducing tension until the urges mount again to an uncontrollable level. The *id* is the center of unconscious drives, while the *ego* is supposed to prevent a person from enacting socially unacceptable desires. The ego represents "willpower" or society's rules that teach people to delay gratification and suppress the id's desires. The *superego*, or conscience, creates guilt when the ego loses control over the id. Because people are not allowed by the ego to enact the id's wishes, sexual and aggressive needs sometimes escape inadvertently into dreams or verbal "Freudian slips." According to psychoanalytic theory, adolescents are motivated by innate drives that the poorly developed ego is not able to control. Once the adolescent satisfies the desire, however, behavior should return to a normal state. Sports, for example, should calm adolescents by draining their aggressive impulses. Channeling sexual or aggressive drives into socially approved activities is another option. For instance, youngsters can put their energy into art projects in order to divert attention from their sexual and aggressive drives.

One of the major shortcomings of psychoanalytic theories is that they virtually ignore the environment's impact on human conduct. Psychologists know, for instance, that aggression depends on cultural training, poverty, rewards, and modeling, not on innate drives. There is also evidence that behaving aggressively increases aggression, rather than diminishing the drive as Freud predicts. Another weakness is that psychoanalysts cannot prove their theories experimentally. Their conclusions come from patients who seek help for various problems, and not from normal adolescents. Psychoanalysts try to explain motivation by delving into the past and searching for unconscious drives that direct the adolescent's present behavior. By the 1930s, psychoanalytic theories were losing popularity. But contemporary psychoanalysts still contend that motivation stems from unconscious drives within the individual.

Drive Theory

From the 1930s until about 1950, drive theories were the most popular explanations for motivation. Drive theorists argued that biological drives, such as hunger, and learned drives, such as fear, motivated people. Drive theorists still thought, however, that a person was driven by unsatisfied, internal needs. The theory essentially ignored a person's power to think and plan. The theories were tested almost exclusively on rats and gave way to better explanations of human motivation in the 1940s.

Field Theory

Kurt Lewin and other psychologists formulated field theories, which assume that environmental forces and internal drives motivate people. The internal drives, however, are not just related to biological needs of survival, as the psychoanalysts and drive theorists assumed. Field theorists said that people learn different values from their environments, so everyone is attracted to different goals by a variety of incentives. Individuals have the power to make intentional decisions and to process information in a variety of unique ways. Cognitive processes, not internal drives, influence people's behavior. Field theories were the pioneers of *cognitive psychology*. A field theorist might say, for example, that students are motivated to read by curiosity (a drive) and by the enticing subject of a book (environment).

Rather than analyzing the past like psychoanalysts, field theorists study an individual's perceptions of situations in the present. Field theorists realize, however, that perceptions of a situation are sometimes a far cry from reality. People are motivated by their personal interpretations of incidents or phenomena, thus field theory is also called *phenomenology* or *Gestalt psychology*. A "gestalt" is literally a figure people can perceive in several ways (see accompanying illustration). Some people will perceive a black vase against a white background. Others will perceive two silhouettes against a black background. In a similar way, people perceive complex situations differently. One adolescent may act aggressively because she interprets an incident in class to mean that the teacher dislikes her. But another student may see that the teacher has a headache and is

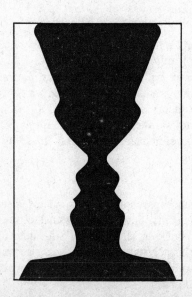

merely being quiet around everyone. Nevertheless, the student's personal perception ultimately determines her conduct. The field theories do demonstrate that personal interpretations of experiences play a vital role in human motivation.

Achievement Theory

Between 1950 and 1970, Richard Atkinson and David McClelland added a new drive to the list of what might motivate students—the drive to achieve. Achievement theorists believe that academic motivation comes from an achievement drive which each culture teaches young children. One student is more motivated than another because the culture successfully instilled the achievement drive in him during childhood. (The theory does not apply to females.) To be motivated, a male must believe that he has a chance to be rewarded for his achievements. A test, the Thematic Apperception Test, was developed to measure the strength of a male's achievement drive. Males with a strong drive supposedly delay gratification, choose tasks of intermediate difficulty, and assume personal responsibility for their success and failure. Achievement theorists conducted programs to train boys to be more achievement oriented, with minimal success except for those with IQ scores over 120 from rich families. The test, however, does not predict a female or minority person's achievement, nor does it predict grades very successfully. The theory itself ignores the fact that a person's motivation varies according to the situation or task at hand. Achievement theories have given way to more convincing explanations of motivation.

Attribution Theory

The major explanations for human motivation since the 1950s are social learning theories and attribution theories. Attribution theorists, such as Frietz Heider and Bernard Weiner, believe that humans have a need to determine the causes of all events. Like field theorists, attribution theorists say that individuals' perceptions of a situation motivate them. People decide what their chances are of attaining certain goals and rewards, even though the decision may be based on an inaccurate perception. For example, students may attribute their poor grades to a prejudiced teacher and consequently be "unmotivated" to study. In reality the cause of the poor grades may be the students' refusal to complete the homework that prepares them for exams. Field theorists and attribution theorists share the belief that perceptions of situations determine how an adolescent will be motivated to behave.

Social Learning Theory

Social learning theory states that motivation is a consequence of the environment, not of internal drives. The theory develops from *behavioral psychology*, which states that motivation depends on rewards. Social learning theorists assume that people decide what to attend to, choose between reinforcing and nonreinforcing options, and develop expectations about rewards in the future. Motivation, however, is not a stable characteristic that remains constant across all situations. Genetic factors may set limits on a person's ultimate abilities, but motivation is primarily created by the environment. For example, students are motivated by rewards they believe are attainable. If they have received rewards in the past, they will be motivated in most academic situations because they have formed expectations for success. Students have the cognitive power to choose goals, to ignore certain rewards in favor of others, and to imitate people they respect. Social learning theorists tell teachers and parents to create adolescent motivation by changing aspects of the environment and not by dwelling on unconscious needs or drives.

Humanistic Psychology

Humanistic psychology arose in the 1960s, lead by Carl Rogers and Abraham Maslow. Humanistic psychologists believe that all humans have an innate drive to "self-actualize." Self-actualized people are "fully functioning" souls who live creatively, develop their potential, and are self-accepting, self-aware, spontaneous, curious, and insightful. Rogers and Maslow contend that if adolescents are left alone, their natural drive to "self-actualize" will motivate them to achieve and to behave appropriately. To become self-actualized a person needs "unconditional positive regard," which means complete acceptance from others. Maslow also says that humans are instinctively motivated to fulfill specific needs: biological, safety, love, self-esteem, and self-actualization. As adolescents meet each need in this hierarchy, they are independently motivated to fulfill the next higher level. Humanistic psychologists use self-concept tests to measure self-actualization.

The shortcomings of humanistic psychology are numerous. Given the vagueness of such terms as "self-actualization" and the unreliability of self-concept tests, there is no way to validate the theory. Humanistic psychologists say that self-actualization is an innate drive in all people, yet they ignore the evidence that many individuals do not manifest any signs of this supposed drive. Indeed, some people even seem to have a natural inclination toward evil acts when left on their own. Humanistic psychologists study values and ideals, but do not provide experimentally sound explanations for human motivation or achievement.

THE IDEAL THEORY OF MOTIVATION

Why can't the experts tell us which of the theories is most relevant for motivating adolescents? One reason is that some theories are only intended to explain one facet of human conduct, such as aggression or fear. Consequently, research cannot always contribute information about normal adolescents. Remember, too, that many researchers exclude adolescents from their experiments. In addition, a theory often offers only a partial explanation for behavior, so we have to extract ideas from several viewpoints. For example, behaviorists are correct that some students will study math instead of watching television only if the reinforcement is powerful enough. But social learning theorists are also right in arguing that some students will do their math in an effort to imitate someone they respect.

People who construct theories and direct research are also human enough to err. Research designs may have methodological flaws that make the results contradictory, tentative, or limited. For instance, few studies determine the impact of a particular method on students over an extended period of time. Also researchers commonly use the average score from a group to prove each theory. This can conceal important information about a technique's success for a particular individual. Some conclusions also come from laboratory experiments that do not replicate the actual situations teachers or parents confront with adolescents.

Inevitably some adults will attack the weaknesses of researchers in order to justify their not reading "those foolish books written by ivory tower intellectuals." Sometimes this judgment is a fair one. Still, as the

methods in the following chapters demonstrate, many dedicated researchers have developed practical techniques from theories that have repeatedly helped adolescents with their academic and social problems. Will
we try them?

Questions for Discussion and Review

1. Why should taxpayers worry about adolescent underachievement?
2. What is your definition of *underachievement*?
3. How have you misdiagnosed someone's motivation or potential?
4. What methods can you suggest for deciding whether or not an adolescent is unmotivated or is truly fulfilling his or her potential?
5. How prevalent is academic underachievement in America?
6. What are your feelings about the effectiveness of public and private
   schools?
7. How do most adolescents feel about school?
8. What could you do to raise the self-esteem of an adolescent who is
   failing several courses and is unpopular with his or her peers?
9. How do you think intelligence tests should be used?
10. What are five questions representing the culture in which you were
    raised that might be appropriate on an intelligence test?
11. How would each of the theoretical views of motivation explain an
    adolescent's aggression in the community or apathy at school?
12. Which theories of motivation best explain your own academic and
    athletic performance?
13. What theories of motivation do the most effective adults whom you
    know seem to be using with adolescents?
14. What are the weaknesses of each theoretical explanation of human
    motivation?

High school counselor to youth: "Your vocational aptitude test indicates
that your best opportunities lie in a field where your parents hold influential positions."

chapter two

Decreasing adolescents' feelings of powerlessness

LOCUS OF CONTROL ATTITUDES

Some adolescents feel alienated and powerless at home and at school.[1] These youngsters doubt their ability to control their own lives and may believe that any effort to improve their unhappy circumstances is fruitless. Although not all adolescents share this sense of powerlessness, many underachieving or disruptive youth do. They may be the victims of an attitude known as *external locus of control*. To motivate these youngsters, we first need to alter their fundamental feelings of powerlessness.

Some evidence indicates that adolescents' beliefs about who controls the future are more reliable predictors of academic achievement than their school's facilities, teachers' qualifications, or student-teacher ratio.[2] Some students who feel powerless may indeed be at the mercy of circumstances beyond their control, such as a prejudiced teacher, a psychologically disturbed parent, a poorly designed school curriculum, or a violent neighborhood. But sometimes adolescents exaggerate their powerlessness because they have not learned to recognize how their own conduct influences their fate. For example, students might complain that there's no use trying, despite the fact that their grades improve when they devote time to studying, or they might think that their teachers are prejudiced against them, ignoring their own bad conduct in class.

Locus of control attitudes determine the adolescent's feelings about who or what controls personal success and failure.[3] Adolescents with an *internal locus of control* believe that their failures are the result of factors that are within their control: not studying, staying up too late the night before the test, or choosing the wrong friends. Those with *external locus of control* orientations blame their poor performances on sources beyond their control: unfair test questions, a prejudiced teacher, bad luck, fate, the weather. Adolescents who believe that external sources account for their failures also refuse to accept personal credit for success: "I only won the track meet because the coach wasn't on my back." "I only passed that test because Tuesday was a lucky day for me." In contrast, youngsters who are internally oriented assume responsibility for their circumstances: "I passed the test because I studied hard." "I lost the meet because I didn't have the good sense to eat extra carbohydrates." Most middle-class Caucasian Americans attribute success and failure to their own innate abilities, effort, and the difficulty of the task. Some other American cultures, however, believe that patience, unity, tact, or fate determine results.

The most difficult youngsters to motivate are those who believe that the future is determined by permanent, uncontrollable characteristics within themselves. It is less debilitating to believe that a bad math grade is due to lack of effort than to lack of intelligence. But many youngsters fail to see the external circumstances or conduct that could be changed to improve their lives.

THE LOCUS OF CONTROL QUESTIONNAIRE

We can measure locus of control attitudes with a questionnaire (Table 2). Most adolescents score from twelve to sixteen points on the test, with delinquents occasionally having scores as high as twenty points. Extremely high scores show that the youngster may not feel personally responsible for success or failure. However, extremely low scores are also problematic. Adolescents with low scores may be unnecessarily blaming or crediting themselves for outcomes that are truly beyond their control. For example, athletes who chastise themselves for a loss when the other team over-

TABLE 2. Locus of Control Questionnaire

yes	1. Do you believe that most problems will solve themselves if you just don't fool with them?
yes	2. Are you often blamed for things that just aren't your fault?
yes	3. Do you feel that most of the time it doesn't pay to try hard because things never turn out right anyway?
no	4. Do you feel that most of the time parents listen to what their children have to say?
yes	5. When you get punished, does it usually seem it's for no good reason at all?
yes	6. Most of the time, do you find it hard to change a friend's opinion?
yes	7. Do you feel that it's nearly impossible to change your parent's mind about anything?
yes	8. Do you feel that when you do something wrong there's very little you can do to make it right?
yes	9. Do you believe that most students are just born good at sports?
yes	10. Do you feel that one of the best ways to handle most problems is just not to think about them?
yes	11. Do you feel that when a student your age decides to hit you, there's little you can do to stop him or her?
yes	12. Have you felt that when people were mean to you it was usually for no reason at all?
no	13. Most of the time, do you feel that you can change what might happen tomorrow by what you do today?
yes	14. Do you believe that when bad things are going to happen they just are going to happen no matter what you try to do to stop them?
yes	15. Most of the time, do you find it useless to try to get your own way at home?
yes	16. Do you feel that when somebody your age wants to be your enemy there's little you can do to change matters?
yes	17. Do you usually feel that you have little to say about what you get to eat at home?
yes	18. Do you feel that when someone doesn't like you there's little you can do about it?

TABLE 2. Locus of Control Questionnaire (continued)

yes	19. Do you usually feel that it's almost useless to try in school because most other children are just plain smarter than you are?
no	20. Are you the kind of person who believes that planning ahead makes things turn out better?
yes	21. Most of the time, do you feel that you have little to say about what your family decides to do?

Note: Each of the answers given here indicates an external attitude.

Source: S. Nowicki and B. Strickland, "Locus of Control Scale for Children," Journal of Consulting and Clincal Psychology, 40 (1973) pp. 148-54. Copyright 1973 by the American Psychological Association. Reprinted by permission of the author.

whelmingly outweighed and outsized theirs are probably too internally oriented and are blaming themselves unjustly. Similarly, students who attribute their victory on a math exam solely to their own intelligence, while ignoring the fact that they were coached by the school's most talented teacher, are also too internally oriented. The ideal attitude is one that is neither too internal nor too external. In other words, "Grant me the serenity to accept the things I cannot change, the courage to change the things I can, and the wisdom to know the difference."

CAUSES AND CONSEQUENCES
OF FEELING POWERLESS

Locus of control seems to relate closely to academic and social conduct.[4] Many underachieving and disruptive youngsters have external locus of control beliefs. These adolescents often lack self-confidence, are dependent on immediate gratification, and are easily discouraged by failure. Often lacking in interpersonal skills, these young people are alienated from their parents, unpopular with their teachers, and involved in delinquency. Adults enjoy working with students who exert effort, so youngsters with an internal locus of control attitude are advantaged.

Although locus of control attitudes do not result from any single cause, several circumstances seem to influence their development. Most externally oriented adolescents have encountered frequent failure and have received very little reinforcement for appropriate conduct and accomplishments. Physical handicaps, learning disabilities, the absence of a father in the home, or authoritarian or overprotective parents also may contribute to a sense of powerlessness. Growing older usually strengthens the belief in personal control for white males, but not for minorities or females. Students who succeed when almost everyone else fails generally develop an internal locus of control, while those who fail while their classmates succeed usually develop external attitudes. If everyone fails or succeeds together, the outcome is usually blamed on the difficulty of the task and not on individual effort or ability: "Since we all made A's, it must have been an easy test." Feelings of powerlessness increase when there are discrepancies between present and past performances: "I always make C's in algebra, so why did I make an A this time?" Adolescents who receive rewards inconsistently also tend to believe in external control. For instance, if Jane always studies hard for her exams but only reaps the benefit of a good grade periodically, she is likely to blame external circumstances for her fate. However, if her exam grades steadily improve, Jane will probably believe that her own effort and ability are responsible. Unfortunately, if the rewards become random and inconsistent again, she will probably regress to her former feelings of powerlessness.

External locus of control is also called *learned helplessness*.[5] When they are convinced that they cannot alter events, many adolescent girls and boys behave helplessly. They may initially seem assertive or hostile: "I am not going to read that stupid book." But apathy, passivity, and helplessness eventually follow: "I don't want to try out for the team." "I can't do this assignment." The more important the task, the greater the likelihood that adolescents will feel helpless if they fail. The quality of work and persistence at a task decrease rapidly with each repeated failure.

But how does the theory of learned helplessness account for someone who seems more determined and more motivated than ever following failure? If the person has a history of success, he or she may decide that a problem can still be remedied and will try again. A student might also be optimistic enough to believe that all failure is a temporary condition. Feeling helpless may even depend on how foreseeable or predictable an outcome was. The youngster who is forewarned about failure usually feels less helpless than the one who is caught completely off guard.

TECHNIQUES FOR IMPROVING
LOCUS OF CONTROL ATTITUDES

Adults in the school, home, and community cannot be expected to counteract all of the forces that might be affecting an adolescent's locus of control attitude, but many effective teaching and counseling techniques have been developed to help adolescents who feel powerless.[6]

Praise

The simplest, least expensive, and most effective technique is to reinforce adolescents consistently when they succeed. When rewarding young people, be consistent, be immediate, and use tangible rewards if praise is ineffective. Reinforcement and contingency contracting (see Chapter 4) improve the academic achievement of many adolescents with a high external locus of control.

Awareness Training

In addition to praise, adolescents who feel powerless should receive training that teaches them to recognize the relationship between their efforts and the consequences. Some adolescents may refuse to discuss their academic or social problems because they are afraid to discover whether or not they actually have the ability to improve unpleasant situations. One remedy for this avoidance is to state the relationship between effort and outcome to the adolescent: "You failed at this task because you didn't practice beforehand, not because you don't have enough ability." This method encourages adolescents to attribute their failures to temporary, controllable factors rather than to permanent characteristics. We can also ask specific questions: "Did you win the race because you trained well or because of good luck?" "Why do you think you passed the test this time?" We can lead class discussions that are designed to help everyone identify the specific habits that improve grades, rather than reinforcing beliefs about the fickleness of fate.

Reality Therapy

Some adolescents learn to accept personal responsibility for resolving their problems by using *reality therapy*.[7] In reality therapy the counselor, teacher, or parent discusses seven questions with the adolescent: "What are you doing?" "How is your conduct helping you?" "How is your conduct helping the teacher (your father, other students, your friends)?" "What can you do to remedy this situation?" "What kind of plan can we both agree to?" "Are you willing to commit yourself to this plan?" "When can you talk with me again to determine the effectiveness of this plan?" A contract outlining the plan is then signed by the adult and the adolescent. Verbal contracts are also acceptable but are far more likely to be misunderstood and quarreled about. A written contract may be simple and direct, but should still be signed by both parties:

> If my brother and I do not have any arguments at home this week, mom will extend my curfew on Saturday night. Mom and Elmer, October 13, 1981

The discussion in Reality Therapy must focus solely on the present conflict and not on problems from the past. There should be no label attached to the youngster's conduct. The problem should simply be described in terms of the behavior: "You do not begin your work without your father forcing you. Let's devise a plan to remedy that." "You talk back to your teacher belligerently whenever she asks you to sit down or be quiet. We need to discuss ways to change that conduct" (see Tables 4 and 5). This is a far cry from asserting, "You are a belligerent, delinquent person who obviously needs help with your lack of motivation and discipline." Talking about the past and asking why the event occurred encourages adolescents to blame their behavior on external sources. The goal is to design a contract in which the adolescent agrees to change some aspects of his or her behavior.

Transactional Analysis

Transactional Analysis shares a common goal with reality therapy by encouraging adolescents to assume personal control over unpleasant circumstances.[8] Teaching young adults to use Transactional Analysis helps them to understand the relationship between their comments and other's responses to them. The adolescent learns how to decide whether a comment represents the perspective of a parent (authoritarian), a child (emotional), or an adult (rational). For example, an adolescent speaking from a child's perspective might say, "I hate you for giving me this work and you're a horrible teacher!" The teacher's retort might represent the perspective of a child and a parent, "I'm in charge here (parent) so you can just get out!" (child). In order to prevent hostile encounters, Transactional Analysis teaches adolescents how to rephrase their comments into a rational form: "This assignment is frustrating me and is making me feel stupid. Can you tell me how to do it?" The most productive interactions occur when both people assume responsibility for stating their feelings and needs candidly without insults. Transactional Analysis also teaches adults and adolescents to recognize the "games" they are playing with each other:[9]

"Uproar": Susan stockpiles all of the real and imagined insults she believes Ms. Smith has been sending her. When she collects enough, she feels justified in creating an uproar in front of everyone.

"Persecutors and Rescuers": George categorizes all adults into two groups—those who are out to persecute him and those who are patsies, pushovers, and helpers. With persecutors he tries to play "victim" and with rescuers he plays the role of "poor me."

"Make Me": Laura wants the teacher to assume responsibility for her, so she encourages Ms. Snodgrass to say, "What *I* want you to do is ———." Instead, the teacher refuses to play the game and says, "If *you* choose to make an A, you may do ———."

In each of these games adolescents are trying to blame external factors for their circumstances. They are relinquishing their personal control and denying their own power. By discussing these games with adolescents or by simply refusing to participate, we can help them discover their power to resolve problems.

Values Clarification

Like Reality Therapy and Transactional Analysis, *values clarification* teaches adolescents how to attain their goals by changing their own conduct.[10] Values clarification activities require youngsters to identify their values, enumerate concrete alternatives for attaining personal goals, evaluate the consequence of each alternative, and commit themselves to one option. The process assumes that adolescents can learn to exert more control over their own lives if they are given a chance to analyze their values and to enact their own goals. The activities are varied, but the questions focus on the relationship between personal conduct and outcomes:

1. Did you act on any of your values this week? What did you do?
2. Did you do anything this week that required more than three solid hours of work?
3. What, if anything, did you do this week that you are proud of?
4. Did you work on any plans this week for some future experience you hope to have?
5. List one or two ways you could have made your week better.
6. Were you in emphatic agreement or disagreement with anyone this week?

Some students who participate in values clarification exercise do begin to recognize the relationship between their values, their actions, and their fate.[11]

Origin Training

Richard DeCharms increases adolescents' feelings of personal power by teaching them to behave as *origins* rather than *pawns*.[12] A pawn is a person who feels pushed around and helpless, but an origin feels in control of his or her life. Pawns often have defensive, defeatist, anxious, or dependent attitudes; origins are confident, optimistic, and independent. Origins have an internal locus of control, while pawns have an external orientation. The teachers in DeCharms's program learn how to help their students change from pawns into origins. Youngsters learn to set their own goals, to self-record their progress, and to observe changes in their behavior. Students spend twenty minutes daily completing activities in an "Origin Manual." These exercises are very similar to those used in values clarification: "What are your goals?" "What have you done today to help you accomplish these goals?" "When have you conducted yourself like an origin rather than like a pawn?" The students also write stories whose characters assume personal responsibility for their lives. Teachers discuss the value of independence and self-control, while providing opportunities for students to make independent choices. Without being authoritarian the teachers avoid being too permissive until students learn to establish their own goals successfully. Teachers explain the rationale underlying every rule so that nobody feels arbitrarily pushed around.

The results of DeCharms's project are encouraging. Most participants learn to set goals and to match their goals more appropriately with their actual abilities. Some improved academically and others reduced their truancy and tardiness. Boys benefited more from the training than girls, and those with external locus of control attitudes benefited more than their peers with internal attitudes. DeCharms concludes that although the changes in attitudes occur slowly, we can help adolescents become more internally oriented.

Structured Environments

Although classes with less structure and more opportunities for independence are appealing, this is not the most beneficial environment for youth who feel helpless. We create a more humane, motivating environment for externally oriented youngsters by providing explicit guidelines and behavioral objectives. Instead of saying, "Choose anything you would like to read from the library and turn in some type of project in ten days," we might suggest, "Choose one book of about one hundred pages from this selection of nonfiction and write a four-page summary by the end of the week". Externally oriented students may also perform better when adults give them feedback on the quality of their performance. In contrast, internally oriented students sometimes do better if they are allowed to judge the correctness of their own work rather than relying on adult approval.

Peer Tutoring

Tutoring younger children may also benefit adolescents who feel controled by external sources. By showing other students how to improve their skills, adolescents sometimes understand that they, too, have the power to influence their fate. The adolescent's advice to the younger child boomerangs and hits the target right between the eyes.

Cooperative Classes

Although myths surrounding the value of competition die hard, competition usually magnifies feelings of helplessness and excessive self-incrimination. We increase youngsters' feelings of personal control by rewarding their efforts, not just by evaluating their performance in comparison to others: "Leroy, don't worry about how many math problems Herman has completed, just notice how many you have finished by working so hard all period." "Team, let's not keep score this afternoon. Instead we'll notice the number of different styles of shooting you are using." Helpless youngsters need success and cooperation, not failure and competition, to begin feeling powerful.

Special Approaches
for Black and Female Adolescents

Most locus of control researchers have studied white males. But studies that include blacks and females show us some unique differences. White female adolescents are more likely than their white male peers to attribute their failures and successes to external sources—luck, helpful friends, or easy tasks.[13] Caucasian women often underestimate their abilities and overestimate contributions from others. White males, on the other hand, are apt to attribute their successes to their own ability and effort. White men with internal locus of control scores are generally successful students. But many successful female students have external locus control attitudes. This difference between white males and females seems to be a consequence of sex role stereotypes. Most young white women are still socialized to be dependent and unassertive, to relinquish control to others, and to achieve happiness vicariously through the achievements of loved ones. To believe she has power over her own decisions and to assertively pursue her goals is to be "unfeminine." Femininity is often at odds with an internal locus of control.

Black women, however, are less likely to have to choose between femininity and an internal locus of control. Many black females are internally oriented because their concept of femininity includes self-direction and individual initiative. Realizing that racial discrimination may still deprive them of control over their lives, many black youngsters nevertheless maintain a positive self-image. In any case, black males and white females are more likely to be externally oriented than white males.[14]

In our own teaching and counseling we may inadvertently be contributing to female or minority youth's feelings of powerlessness by reinforcing racial and sex role stereotypes of passive personalities. We should acquaint minority and female adolescents with heroines and heroes who exhibit personal control over their lives. We can also remind minorities and females of their talents and power, and we can encourage adolescent women to examine fears about being "unfeminine." By redefining *femin-*

inity, we show them that assertiveness, ambition, and initiative are desirable human traits. Being active in sports also creates more internal attitudes for some young women.[15]

Caution! We do a disservice to minorities and girls if we make them believe that their personal efforts will always yield rewards. Because sexism and racism do sometimes deprive these individuals of control over their fate, we must help them distinguish between failure caused by prejudice and failure they create themselves. Locus of control training must not pretend that the powerlessness of females and minorities is never a consequence of prejudice.

ADULT MODELS

Adults who sincerely desire to empower adolescents with an internal locus of control can present themselves as models. Adults who present themselves as downtrodden, helpless victims are in no position to expect adolescents to assume responsibility for their own circumstances. "Do as I say, not as I do" is feeble advice. We need to be aware of the impact that our statements might have on adolescents who already feel that external sources control people. Some statements reinforce the idea that everyone is powerless: "There's nothing we teachers can do to get that principal to leave us alone." "I was late to work yesterday because my luck ran out with the car." Statements that represent internal control are more likely to benefit adolescents: "I haven't figured out a way yet, but I know that somehow we can persuade the principal to change the policy." "I am going to talk with my supervisor and identify exactly what I need to do to get a pay raise next fall."

Adults in the adolescent's life can demonstrate that humans do have the personal power to control many circumstances. Perhaps our modeling will persuade young people to try molding their own destinies, rather than buckling under by believing in external control.

Questions for Discussion and Review

1. How can you help yourself to develop more internal locus of control attitudes?
2. In what situations have you been most profoundly affected by your own locus of control attitude?

3. How can an excessively internal locus of control attitude be detrimental?

4. What counseling techniques could you implement to improve underachievers' external attitudes?

5. What contributes to an external locus of control attitude?

6. Why is just providing success and praise insufficient to create internal locus of control attitudes?

7. Why might many blacks and females feel more powerless than white males?

8. How could you help minority and female adolescents develop more internal attitudes while discouraging unjust self-incrimination?

9. What are ten educational practices that could contribute to adolescents' feelings of powerlessness and helplessness?

10. Why should locus of control attitudes concern teachers or counselors?

11. What are the essential questions in Reality Therapy?

12. Other than the suggestions in this chapter, how do you think an adolescent's feelings of helplessness might be overcome?

13. How does Transactional Analysis help an adolescent gain more control in conversations?

14. What are some favorite "games" you have played with your teachers?

15. How are Reality therapy and values clarification alike?

16. Which methods for encouraging an internal locus of control appeal most to you?

17. Which of your own adolescent friends have locus of control attitudes that seem to impede their progress? How might you help them?

chapter three

Motivating adolescents academically

THE REFORM OF SECONDARY EDUCATION

Can we motivate adolescents without expensive programs? The good news is that the most expensive educational innovations do not usually yield greater academic benefits than the least costly methods. The 1978 National Commission on the Reform of Secondary Education concluded that many inexpensive changes in secondary schools improve adolescents' achievement.[1] The Commission recommends that all attempts to motivate adolescents through reforms in secondary schools include the students and their parents, not just educators. How many of the Commission's suggestions are your school using?

1. Define the school's goals and specify the criteria for grading students. Publish and publicize these in the form of *behavioral activities*.
2. Involve the community in the school's activities.
3. Revise and revitalize the curriculum.
4. Train teachers to use a variety of instructional styles.
5. Design a curriculum and flexible schedules that permit students to take advantage of off-campus career opportunities.
6. Provide more extensive vocational training.

7. Create job placement services in the school.
8. Educate students more fully in world affairs.
9. Provide alternative schools in lieu of the traditional eight-to-three daytime program.
10. Award credit for learning and experience that occur outside the school building.
11. Develop an exam system similar to college entrance exams to determine fitness for entry into courses.
12. Study the influence of television as an instructional tool and expand its use in education.
13. Develop better communication between secondary and postsecondary educators. Eliminate grade point average and class rank as the only admissions criteria for colleges.
14. Develop security plans that will safeguard students while they are in the school building.
15. Keep accurate records of serious assaults in order to design preventive programs.
16. Distribute a code of students' rights and obligations, including suspension procedures.
17. Create a student-faculty committee to decide issues of liability and censorship for the school newspaper.
18. Maintain the students' privacy in school records.
19. Abolish corporal punishment.
20. Abolish academic success as a prerequisite for participation in school activities.
21. Abolish compulsory attendance beyond the age of fourteen.
22. Provide everyone with fourteen years of free education beyond kindergarten.
23. Disassociate the National Association of Secondary School Principals from the National Honor Society and the National Student Council Association.
24. Eliminate all forms of sexism and racism in counseling, sports, teaching, curriculum, and books.

INDIVIDUALIZED INSTRUCTION

An additional way to motivate adolescents is through individualized instruction. Fortunately, many techniques for individualizing instruction do not demand much more time than conventional teaching.[2] One simple way to individualize a curriculum is to present material visually, orally, and kinesthetically. Students can then choose the mode that suits them best (Table 3). John might prefer to learn verb conjugations by writing exercises in his book (visual mode), Sandy might use a cassette tape (aural mode), and Jill might repeat verbs aloud to a classmate who corrects her mistakes (oral and aural modes). Providing several modes is possible with learning centers, learning activity packages, or contingency contracts. In learning centers several different activities are available in designated areas of the classroom, but the educational objective is still the same for all students. At one center people might be watching a video-cassette about the short vowel sounds, while at other centers classmates are playing board games or completing puzzles or written exercises that teach these same vowels. Students are free to choose the activities that help them learn most effectively. A "lap", learning activity package, follows the same principle. A learning activity package states the goals of the daily lesson and provides several options students may pursue to achieve these goals.

Commercially published programmed materials and teaching machines also tailor a curriculum to individuals' abilities and speeds. A

TABLE 3. Learning Styles and Instructional Methods

Primarily Auditory	*Primarily Visual*
Students read aloud	Films
Teacher explains the lesson	Flash cards
Teacher lectures	Notes on board
Students make speeches	Written exercises
Students listen to tapes	Programmed materials
Teacher plays a record	Silent reading
	Written projects
Primarily Oral	*Primarily Kinesthetic*
Debates	Role playing
Responding to tapes	Building mobiles
Responding to questions	Playing board games
Class discussions	Laboratory experiments
	Using cuisinaire rods
	Acting out plays

diagnostic test identifies each adolescent's skills, then the lessons are assigned to each person at the appropriate level of mastery. Learners advance at their own pace to the more complicated lessons in the series. Programmed materials do not prevent the teacher from instructing the whole class together, from using peer tutors, or from exposing everyone to the same films, laboratory experiments, or group discussions. As students work on their own programmed lessons, the teacher is free to tutor them individually or in small groups.

Independent study is another approach to individualizing instruction. When given choices, most adolescents choose tasks of intermediate difficulty and do not establish ridiculously simple goals.[3] During independent study students should have the opportunity to earn respectable grades based on their success with materials at their level. When the abilities of students in the same class are significantly different, individualized standards of grading are more motivating than a system that permanently excludes the less skilled from rewards.

Finally, adults can individualize a curriculum by providing a little additional time for learners who work slowly. In several studies, slower learners attained all the academic objectives when given only 10 to 20 percent more time.[4] There are ways for teachers to create additional time in their own classes: Adults can give students the option of continuing to work beyond the designated deadline with a minimal academic penalty, or they can let faster workers pursue other activities while their slower classmates continue working. Peer tutoring also equalizes some differences in students' pace or abilities. Faster workers can help slower ones, with academic and social benefits for both.

LEARNING STYLES

Another aspect of motivating adolescents is considering their individual learning styles. More than twenty dimensions of learning styles have been identified, convincing some educators that completely individualized instruction is impossible.[5] Some school systems, however, have tried to match the adolescent's own learning style with the teacher's techniques. Students are questioned before being assigned a teacher to determine whether they prefer working alone or with others, with or without adult supervision, and with books or nonprinted materials. Some adults even suggest that in the future information on each student's learning style will be kept in his or her dossier, thereby allowing a marriage of learners and teachers who are educationally suited for each other. On the other hand, some educators argue that we should not always teach adolescents according to their preferred or strongest styles, but that we should help them develop their weaker modes. One compromise to this dilemma is to teach very difficult skills in the student's best style, and to improve their weakest styles with simpler tasks.

How can we identify an adolescent's learning style? A reasonable approach is to ask the student to answer some questions, explaining that the goal is to discover which teaching method will be most motivating: "What distracts you as you work?" "What do you do to warm up before studying?" "Do you work best alone, with a peer tutor, with the teacher's help, or in a small group with your classmates?" "Do you understand material best when you hear it, read it, watch a visual presentation, talk about it yourself, or perform an experiment?" "Do you work best in the classroom or in some other place?" "What do teachers or classmates do that helps you learn?" "What materials do you need to make your work easier?" "Do you usually take time to think about your answers before responding or do you respond impulsively?"

Some teachers are able to model reflective thinking for their impulsive students and teach them to respond more slowly and deliberately. We can also notice whether the student seems more aware of the similarities between concepts (a *leveler)* or more aware of the contrasts (a *sharpener*). Does the student solve problems best by deducing the correct answer from a general concept, by using programmed materials, and by working with a very structured assignment? If so, he or she is best at *convergent thinking*. Does the student prefer to work alone and create solutions? If so, he or she is best at *divergent thinking*. Is the adolescent easily influenced by others, submissive, overly dependent on external rewards, and frustrated by ambivalent situations? These are characteristics of a *field dependent* learner who functions best in an orderly, supervised class with few demands for self-direction and a great deal of reinforcement. In contrast, the *field independent* learner is more whimsical, self-directed, and disorderly, functioning well in less structured classes. Identifying a student's *cognitive style* can help us select the most effective teaching methods.

CONTRACTS AND MASTERY LEARNING

Adolescents who are disruptive or bored often become calm and motivated when adults use *contingency contracts*. Individually guided motivation, mastery learning, individually prescribed instruction, diagnostic-prescriptive teaching, and individualized educational programs are based on the principles of contracting.[6] Those adolescents who use contracts improve their academic achievement and social conduct. Contingency contracts succeed at school, at home, in programs for delinquents, in psychiatric centers, in classes for the retarded or learning disabled, and at work.[7]

Like conventional business contracts, educational contracts are written explanations of each party's obligations and "payments" to the other.[8] First the contract specifies the task the adolescent is expected to perform. If possible, the adolescent should participate in this goal setting, rather than merely being commanded to perform. Many parents and teachers will protest that they have already made their demands clear. Too often, however, adults demand that adolescents "respect," "try harder," "improve," or "be attentive." These are *not* acceptable words for a contingency contract, nor for a business contract. The seller of a house would not write into a contract, "I'll be sure the house is in good condition when you buy it." What precisely does "good condition" mean? The buyer's and seller's views probably differ. When they are writing contracts, adults must use verbs that represent observable, measurable, indisputable behavior. These statements are called *behavioral objectives* (Table 4). A sound house contract would state that the seller "will repair the two holes in the roof and repaint the kitchen before the buyer moves in." Likewise, adults must acquire the habit of observing and naming specific behavior for adolescents, rather than referring to attitudes or vague concepts (Table 5).

The next steps in a contract are stating the conditions under which the goals must be accomplished and designating what *level of mastery* is necessary to earn the rewards. The terms of the contract must be clear. For instance, how long does the adolescent have to achieve the goal? Can the youngster use slide rules, dictionaries, peer assistance, or notes to achieve the goal? The final phase of contracting is to specify the criteria and the payoffs (Table 6).

TABLE 4. Behavioral Statements

Which of the following are correctly written as behavioral statements?

1. Susan does not follow her teacher's direction in class.
2. Susan has no will power or self-discipline.
3. I want my son to try harder at school.
4. Team players who exert the most effort will win a prize.
5. By understanding the cause of the war, students can make a C on the test.
6. We want our children to respect their elders.
7. To earn a good grade you must shoot 8 consecutive baskets in gym class before the end of the six weeks.
8. We want our daughter to listen without interrupting when an older person speaks.
9. I want everyone to come to class before the bell rings.
10. These adolescents have such poor attitudes.

Note: Statements 1, 7, 8, and 9 are behavioral statements.

TABLE 5. Stating Attitudes in Behavioral Terms

Poor Attitude, Uncooperative, Unmotivated	Disruptive
Cuts class	Slams books and doors
Doesn't dress for gym	Tardy to class
Doesn't take opportunity to do makeup work	Leaves desk without permission
Does not bring pencil, paper, or book to class	Runs and shouts in hallways
Makes humorous responses to teacher's serious questions	Throws spitballs, chalk, or books
Does not ask teacher for help	Talks while teacher or peers are talking
Smokes in undesignated areas	Gives ridiculous answers to teacher's questions
Never volunteers answers	Wears a hat in class
	Throws food in cafeteria

TABLE 6. Daily Contract for Academic Skills

Points I earned today	Maximum possible	Activity
2	2	Attending class
5	5	Completing the assigned lesson in class
0	3	Turning in last night's homework
0	5	Making fewer than 3 mistakes on the quiz
		or
2	2	Making fewer than 5 mistakes on the quiz

Daily grading: A = 14 points; B = 12; C = 10; D = 8.

Agreements can either be *proclamations* or *mutual contracts*. Proclamations are written exclusively by an adult, whereas youngsters help design mutual contracts. Contracts are generally more motivating than proclamations and prevent disputes between the parties. If contracts fail to improve an adolescent's conduct, examine the document carefully: Were the objectives written in behavioral terms? Were the conditions, grades, or social incentives specified at the outset? Was the contract written and shared with the youngster? Were the goals set just slightly above the adolescent's present level of performance? Were incentives other than grades provided? Were the rewards given frequently enough? Was the recording accurate and designed to allow adolescents to chart their progress daily? Did the adolescent choose the reward? If the answer to any question is "no," the contract failed because it was poorly designed.

Contracts have advantages seldom found in other motivational strategies. Because contracting requires people to be specific and candid with each other at the outset of their relationship, disputes are less likely to arise over discriminatory treatment. Most adults already have an unwritten contract etched inside their own heads. Contingency contracts are actually just ways of transferring these plans into public, written forms for the youngster's benefit. Contracts also oblige adults who are confused about their objectives for adolescents to formulate and publicize their expectations. Most grownups can write a brief, simple contract in minutes. Colleagues and parents can also share their contracts, multiplying creative options for students.

Some adults protest that contingency contracts are forms of "bribery." But bribery is a payoff for illegal or undesirable acts. Receiving a reward for academic achievements or good conduct is like receiving a monthly paycheck from an employer. A contingency contract is an incentive to keep up the good work. If adolescents complain about differences in their contracts, be candid with them. Explain that not everyone started with exactly the same skills. Ask them if it is fair to start a race by putting some runners fifteen feet in front of others. The same principle applies to academics. If some students are better readers than others, their contracts should differ. With practice and guidance many adolescents eventually become skilled enough to motivate themselves by designing their own contingency contracts (see Chapter 11).

INTRINSIC AND EXTRINSIC REWARDS

Some adolescents simply are not inspired by the curriculum or by grades. These students need nonacademic incentives to maintain their perseverance at taxing or boring tasks. When an activity is not intrinsically pleasurable, people rely on *external*, or *extrinsic, rewards* to force themselves to continue. Society offers us external rewards for the work we do by giving us promotions, paychecks, or special awards such as "best salesperson of the month." These external rewards often motivate people to work at tasks that are not pleasurable or not as appealing as other alternatives. Offering someone who hates math a diploma for completing the required courses or exempting a student from homework for finishing all the problems during class are *external reinforcers* that may cause unmotivated souls to blossom into dynamos.

Using external reinforcement is not a simple task. To begin with, not every adolescent is attracted to the same type of reward. In addition, rewards can lose their value from one day to the next: On Tuesday a student may value peer attention above all else, but on Wednesday a compliment from the coach might be more potent. Most people also lose interest in rewards that are excessively repeated. This is called *satiation.* Adults who are wise enough to motivate adolescents by predicting what will reward them at a particular moment have a real gift. Most teachers who try to anticipate what will attract adolescents guess incorrectly.[9] Rather than try to guess, we can let them select their own rewards. Some young people need immediate, regular reinforcement for almost every achievement, and others can delay gratification and work without much approval from external sources.[10] Underachievers and economically deprived students, for example, often respond better to prompt, *tangible rewards* than to verbal praise or delayed attention.[11] Adults who want to help adolescents achieve their goals will reward them consistently, regularly, and lovingly.

Some critics charge that systematically rewarding adolescents creates an unhealthy dependence on extrinsic reinforcement, undermines the intrinsic potential of the activity itself, and constitutes bribery. ("Youngsters should behave themselves at school because it's morally correct, and not to earn extra minutes at recess." "Students should study because they enjoy the material, not in order to get good grades.") These criticisms of external rewards, however, disregard several crucial issues. First, some adolescents simply will not study or behave without receiving an external incentive. For numerous reasons these students do not find academic work intrinsically rewarding. Does a humane adult simply stand by and allow these youngsters to fail rather than design systematic incentives which help them master academic skills? Behavioral psychologists agree with their critics that if a person already finds an activity inherently motivating, other people should not tamper with this pleasure by adding external incentives.

When adolescents refuse to work voluntarily at academic tasks, we say they are "not motivated." A more accurate description is that, for whatever personal reason, the youngster does not find the task *intrinsically reinforcing.* The unmotivated student is someone who needs an external incentive to work because the assignment itself is not pleasurable. Defining what is intrinsically reinforcing is a matter of personal taste which is probably learned from experiences in the individual's own life. A child whose parents hate sports is probably not going to find basketball intrinsically pleasurable. An adolescent who has continually failed in school is not likely to find any academic task reinforcing. Supportive grownups can help adolescents use external incentives to create motivation for those essential, required tasks that lack intrinsic appeal.

Assume that Ramond is a sophmore in high school who must learn to read at an eighth-grade level if he wants a diploma. Because he is presently such a poor reader, Ramond is short tempered or bored when asked to do the classroom work necessary to learn how to read. Once he becomes a proficient reader, books will probably become intrinsically reinforcing, but in the meantime, Ramond can profit from external incentives to help him persist at tedious assignments. The teacher should reinforce him consistently and frequently for the small improvements in his classwork. This process is called *shaping* behavior by rewarding *successive approximations*. Many adults make the mistake of expecting too much from the adolescent too soon and of being too stingy with external incentives. Ramond needs a *continuous schedule* of reinforcement in the beginning, not random or *intermittent reinforcement*. The continuous schedule can change to a less frequent system of reward after he is able to work independently for longer periods without getting frustrated. To show Ramond his progress, the teacher and he make a written record of his *baseline behavior*. Baseline is the period of time before any external incentives are used. Ramond's baseline charts for two weeks show that he works only ten to fifteen minutes of each class period on his assignments. The ultimate behavioral goal is for him to work for fifty of the sixty minutes in class before the end of the six weeks. The teacher and Ramond discuss the goal, the baseline data, and the relationship between external incentives and academic motivation. The teacher allows Ramond to choose his own reward for each day's improvement of five minutes' additional work in class. The teacher also provides *social reinforcement* by complimenting any improvement and by ignoring him on days when he fails to reach his goal. Both Ramond and the teacher keep daily records of his conduct in class. As the weeks pass, other kinds of rewards begin to accumulate. Ramond begins to feel better about himself because the teacher no longer gripes at him, his grades are improving, his parents are receiving good reports from school, and he notices that he has made progress in reading, which contributes to his status in a society that values literacy. Many adults would say that Ramond is finally motivated. More accurately, Ramond and a supportive adult have arranged external incentives that are helping him master tasks which are not initially rewarding from his personal perspective.

A system that conscientiously rewards adolescents for their academic and social achievements is not any more objectionable than other customs which our culture condones: paychecks and promotions, bonuses and trophies for winning teams, compliments to the chef, or applause for a command performance. In the ideal situation perhaps people would live without the need for any external rewards, driven only by the joy derived from the task itself. Wise adults will certainly wean adolescents from dependence on external rewards by gradually diminishing their frequency as the task itself becomes more pleasant. But until all students find joy in reading, reworking math problems for the third time, sitting quietly through a lecture on a lovely spring day, or missing a championship ball game to study for a test, external incentives will bridge some troubled waters.[12]

THE POWER OF PRAISE

The mere act of praising desirable conduct and academic progress motivates most adolescents.[13] *Praise is probably the most powerful yet the most ignored incentive adults can provide for adolescents!* Underachievers and delinquents are especially sensitive to praise. Even academically talented youngsters are very responsive to it, although some prefer compliments related to their accomplishments rather than to their personal qualities. Sadly, most adults bestow attention, praise, and patience on those who need these gifts least—the achiever.[14]

Praise, however, sometimes backfires. Compliments that sound like evaluation or that pressure youngsters to repeat superior performances create fear or aversion.[15] Verbal compliments may also make some adolescents feel awkward, while others become suspicious of the flatterer's motives. To alleviate these anxieties, we can write compliments in specific, but not exaggerated, form: "Your paper contained many creative ideas," rather than "You are the most superb writer I've met in all my years as a teacher." If adolescents dislike the adult who compliments them, they may act indifferent. But most youngsters will not dislike people who honestly applaud their accomplishments.

Direct compliments are not the only ways to support adolescents. We flatter most youngsters by asking for their opinions and asking them to explain their ideas. We can also send complimentary notes home to parents or brag about an adolescent in front of another adult. Since some teachers inadvertently attend more to students who sit near them, the physical arrangement of the classroom may be influencing who is ignored and who is complimented. Rearranging the seating patterns periodically should eliminate this possibility. Complimenting an adolescent often causes peers to imitate the praiseworthy act. This phenomenon, *vicarious reinforcement*, is additional encouragement for grownups to catch kids being good and then "let them have it"—praise, that is.

GRADES AND COMPETITION

The traditional bunch of grapes dangled in front of adolescents as an external reward is a good grade. Grades are then cashed in for other goodies: diplomas, admission to honor societies, entrance to lucrative careers, or society's approval. The most popular system of grading is to evaluate everyone's performance "on the curve," which is called *norm-referenced grading*. Only a predesignated percentage of the class can earn A's or B's, while the majority earn C's. A student's grade depends on a comparison to the "norm" grade of the entire class and not on the mastery of specified skills. The poor performance of fellow classmates is good fortune because the norm grade is lowered. Some teachers continually raise their grading standards to prevent too many students from earning high grades. Other teachers raise standards to avoid being called "too easy" by their colleagues or administrators. (This shows the adult's need for peer approval.)

Does norm-referenced, competitive grading motivate most adolescents? Many researchers think not. *Criterion-referenced grading*, or *mastery learning*, is usually a much more powerful incentive.[16] In criterion-referenced grading one student's success is not a classmate's loss. The rewards depend on accomplishing the stated objectives regardless of how many other people succeed (see Table 6). Apathetic or disheartened underachievers are especially excited by mastery learning. Failure in competitive situations usually creates shame and anxiety, not motivation. Urban American students are generally more competitive than their classmates from rural or nonwhite cultures, and become more so with age. Yet when they are exposed to cooperative educational practices and grading, most students prefer the noncompetitive approach.

Why, then, is competitive grading still so popular? Some advocates argue that college entrance decisions depend upon competitive high school grades. An eight-year study, however, followed fifteen hundred youngsters from thirty high schools who enrolled in three hundred different colleges solely on the basis of their teachers' recommendations. When socioeconomic status, race, and sex were considered, students from the traditional competitive secondary schools who were admitted to college on the basis of grades did not do better than those from the noncompetitive, high schools.[17] Some adults also believe that competitive, norm-referenced grading prepares adolescents for the "real world" outside school. Competition represents the "survival of the fittest" and "builds character." These beliefs seem to overlook the many endeavors in American society that require cooperation or competition against preestablished criteria rather than agains co-workers. Undeniably prizes are sometimes awarded only to the "top dog," such as the person with the highest sales record for the month. But only those people who are convinced that they have a chance to win are motivated by this kind of competition.

The disadvantages of competitive grading do not mean that we should eliminate all competition from school but rather that we should incorporate more cooperative and individualistic approaches to learning and grading. Competition is appropriate when speed or quantity is the goal or when individuals are simply curious about comparing their abilities. But until someone demonstrates that the pervasive use of competitive grading boosts self-esteem and academic skills, adolescents should be allowed to choose whether they want to compete against or work alongside one another.

LEADERSHIP STYLES

Underachievers are more sensitive to an adult's style of leadership than are achievers.[18] Underachieving and financially deprived youngsters achieve best under the direction of adults who are friendly yet well prepared with structured classroom activites and specific behavioral objectives. The best approach is to solicit adolescents' input into academic matters and to establish friendly relationships, but without relinquishing clear instructional goals.[19] In fact, adolescents who are given too many alternatives and too much liberty are likely to feel frustrated and annoyed.[20] Most people feel happy and free when given a few positively stated options to choose from. For example, "If you turn in your homework, you will have some free time in class tomorrow" makes students feel more free than "If you don't turn in your homework, you will have to do the work tomorrow and lose five points." Likewise, asking students to choose between playing tennis, volleyball, or soccer is less frustrating than asking them what they want to do in gym class for the next semester.

Grownups may wonder how to establish enough power to command attention and obedience without being tyrants who destroy rapport with adolescents. Some leaders are powerful because followers respect their skills and expertise (expert power), others because they have created a personal bond with their followers (referent power). Some gain power merely because followers believe that people in certain roles, like preachers and teachers and politicians, have a legal or moral right to direct others (legitimate power). Finally a person can have *coercive power* based on his or her control over rewards and punishment such as grades, letters of recommendation, and corporal punishment. Our control over adolescents can come from these four sources of power. Expert and referent sources are the most likely to create rapport and respect. The most desirable situation occurs when an athlete obeys her coach's directions because she believes the coach is talented and wise, not because she fears a bad grade. We create referent and expert power by developing competencies that adolescents respect and by establishing genuine friendship with youngsters.

DISCUSSIONS OR LECTURES

Despite democratic intentions, most teachers verbally dominate their classes.[21] The adult is the active person in the class, and the students are passive. However, research repeatedly shows that lectures are not the best way to motivate most students.[22] Students learn most from talking, not from listening. Lectures are only motivating when the speaker is dynamic and inspiring, when the material is not available from another source, when we need a change of pace, when time is too limited for any other activity, or when students request explanations.

Sometimes teachers who invite students to participate are disappointed because everyone remains silent. Or everyone may talk simultaneously without developing any meaningful dialogue. Leading class discussions is an art, not an accident. To begin, we must formulate questions that encourage adolescents to evaluate, speculate, or interpret, not merely to regurgitate facts from the text. Instead of "What were the causes of the war?" ask "Which causes of the war do you think were most foolish?" Don't repeat or interrupt students' responses. Give everyone ample time to think before leaping in and providing the answer to your own questions. Don't reply critically or with a "Yes, but. . ." unless the group is assertive and self-confident enough to ignore an adult's rebuffs. If an answer is incorrect, encourage exploration: "That's not right, but do you have other ideas?" "I see how you might believe that. Does anyone have a different answer?" "I'm not sure I understand. Can you explain a little more?" If students are inattentive to their classmates' comments, repeat each others' remarks, or introduce irrelevant ideas, require them to paraphrase the previous person's comment before speaking: "Jane said the present was wrong, but I believe . . ." Discussions are also more goal oriented and focused when every remark is summarized on the board in abbreviated form. This written procedure allows students to correct themselves and to avoid repeating each other. At the end of an hour an outline of the discussion is on display so the group sees its progress toward a specific goal. If students continue to direct their comments only to the teacher, redirect their statements to classmates: "Sharon, what do you think about Fran's question?"

When hosting a class discussion, seats should be arranged in one or two concentric circles, not in rows. The teacher may sit with the group or wander around casually while maintaining eye contact. To relax students enough to speak out in front of the whole class, begin with smaller group activities that require everyone to speak. If people are particularly meek, support their verbal contributions by awarding academic credit to all participants. Assertiveness training or a self-management project might help the extremely timid souls. Seat the most reticent people near the more verbal ones so that peer modeling can occur. Show videotapes or listen to audiotapes of other adolescents involved in a productive discussion.

Discuss the value of contributing in class and of asking questions about confusing material. Above all, compliment adolescents who risk speaking and chastise anyone who mocks a classmate's questions or comments. With our deliberate assistance, most adolescents can learn to enjoy expressing themselves verbally in productive group discussions.

USES AND ABUSES OF HOMEWORK

Although class discussions are clearly beneficial to most students, some critics wonder about the value of homework. Homework sometimes penalizes or demoralizes adolescents who are employed or who have familial obligations to their own children, siblings, or parents. A quiet, conducive environment for homework is not accessible to all youngsters. Underachievers or students with learning disabilities might also be frustrated by homework that deprives them of assistance or encouragement from knowledgeable adults. Another consideration is that the chance to complete work at home might reduce the incentive to work diligently at school. On the other hand, additional practice at home improves some student's skills and permits relaxed self-pacing without peer pressure or interference. The value of homework, therefore, depends on the environment at home and on the individual's particular learning style and mental abilities.

Perhaps a fair compromise is to devise assignments that allow all students enough time to find a conducive workplace and to get help from teachers or peers. Arrange time during class for students to complete most of their practice exercises. Observe whether homework actually seems to help or to hinder your students. Consider whether your students have study halls or quiet environments at home. Although "practice makes perfect," repeating the same errors without correction and guidance breeds frustration and bad habits.

A MOTIVATING CURRICULUM

Although homework is a questionable device for motivating adolescents, the secondary school curriculum is a more powerful culprit in destroying academic enthusiasm. Many talented adolescents, as well as their less gifted classmates, are bored with their school's curriculum. The recent attempt to change the high school's curriculum "back to basics" has decreed that courses in reading, writing, and mathematics should take precedence over all others because schools have failed to provide these fundamental skills in the curriculum. The advocates of "back to basics" claim that adolescents are falling behind in their basic abilities and that the nation will eventually suffer as a consequence of the efforts to create a contemporary, relevant curriculum. The statistical fact, however, is that adolescents are not underachieving in their fundamental skills but in the more complex, higher-order reasoning skills.[23]

A second issue in creating an appealing curriculum is censorship. Some citizens protest that the content of certain relevant, stimulating books is too sexual, violent, or treatening to "American ideology." Among the books on censors' black lists have been Plato's *Republic* (anti-Christian), Shakespeare's *Macbeth* (too violent), Melville's *Moby Dick* (homosexuality), and E. B. White's *Charlotte's Web* (too candid about death). In 1925 Tennessee even forbade a biology teacher, John Scopes, from teaching Darwin's theory of evolution. Influenced by censors, the curriculum for adolescents has too often ignored contemporary issues like the Vietnam War, sexual conduct, death, racism and sexism, environmental protection, and ethnic studies. Those educators with courage and dedication have, nevertheless, withstood the censors' attacks and created curricular programs to motivate adolescents.

Sometimes a high school's graduating class catches "senioritis." The symptoms are apathy, absenteeism, and restlessness. Anticipation of enrolling in postsecondary training, getting married, or earning money can make many seniors feel that the curriculum in their final year is especially irrelevant. But several school systems have created new alternatives for the boring senior curriculum. Early college admissions or a course offered in the high school for college credit satisfies some youngsters. In 1971 only 2 percent of American secondary schools permitted early college admissions, but by 1979 this figure had increased to 54 percent.[24] Students can also pursue career internships during their senior year, attending classes for half of each day and then leaving campus to work. Travel abroad and independent study are options, as well as tutoring and counseling younger classmates. Volunteer work, such as child care or traffic surveys for the local government, also can give seniors valuable vocational experience in their curriculum.

THE MAGIC OF HUMOR

Why would a serious textbook on adolescent motivation present an insignificant, silly topic like humor? The sober message is that humor does improve academic achievement and social conduct for many adolescents. Adults who are talented enough to joke reciprocally with adolescents often reduce the tension and aggression that impede academic progress. Numerous research studies demonstrate that laughter has the power to create rapport, reduce fear, destroy racial and social barriers, and enhance self-esteem.[25] People who laugh together usually learn to accept each other's limitations and failures. Humor often furnishes a way to enter serious discussions about academic or social problems. Some evidence shows that witty students even enhance a group's academic efficiency and productivity. Humor also seems to facilitate memorizing facts and drawing students' attention to new topics.

Unfortunately humor is a two-edged sword. Adults who joke with adolescents but who balk at mutual teasing usually increase anxiety and hostility in the classroom. Using humor as a weapon, adults sometimes humiliate youngsters who are not in any position to talk back. By mocking their beliefs or customs, these adults send a clear message: "I am superior to you and can criticize you without repercussion." "What's the matter, haven't you got a sense of humor?" is too common a criticism of youngsters who refuse to laugh when they are being made fun of. Although we should all encourage one another to laugh at our own beliefs or characteristics from time to time, humor is only funny when everyone participates equally.

SELF-FULFILLING PROPHECIES

Besides using humor to embarrass adolescents, some adults create debilitating self-fulfilling prophecies for youngsters. A *self-fulfilling prophecy* is a preconceived expectation that effects the way we behave towards an adolescent and thereby causes our initial prophecy to come true.[26] We are often totally unaware of our expectations or of how preconceptions are altering our conduct. In the Oak School Experiment researchers told teachers that certain students were "late bloomers" who would exhibit academic spurts later in the term. In reality all students had the same initial achievement levels and abilities. At the end of the experiment, those youngsters who were labeled as late bloomers had advanced further academically than their classmates. The assumption is that the teachers at Oak School supposedly treated the students differently on the basis of their expectations and caused the prophecies to be fulfilled. The self-fulfilling prophecy is also referred to as the *Pygmalion Effect* in reference to the play, *Pygmalion*. In Shaw's play, a professor with great expectations for a poor, uneducated flower girl treats her in accordance with his prophecy and transforms her into "my fair lady."[27]

Examples of self-fulfilling prophecies are evident in most secondary schools. A beneficent teacher may demand very little from Indian students and excuse their poor achievement as "cultural deprivation." In response, these students will probably continue to perform below their actual potential. On the other hand, a coach who believes that black youngsters are athletically gifted may encourage and train them in such positive ways that the prophecy comes true. Or a counselor who has high expectations for for adolescent girls in math and science courses is far more likely to create future physicians and physicists than one who treats girls as though they were not mathematically minded. Adolescents whom adults believe are bright usually receive more attention, praise, assistance, and patience than those who are labeled less gifted.[28] Teachers often ask simpler questions and lower the academic requirements for students from poor families or ethnic groups. The richer or brighter the student is believed to be, the more likely it is that he or she will be given the benefit of the doubt in ambivalent situations. For example, adults may describe inattentive adolescents in college preparatory classes as "in need of motivation," while labeling the identical conduct in vocational classes as "short attention span and hyperactivity."

Although there is some doubt about the strength of self-fulfilling prophecies, we must nevertheless realize that our preconceptions about any adolescent inevitably alter some of our behavior. Rather than hampering any youngster's academic progress or self-esteem, we should monitor our personal conduct in an effort to create a consistently positive prophecy for all adolescents.

Questions for Discussion and Review

1. Which recommendations of the Commission on Secondary Education do you believe would most influence adolescents' motivation? Why?
2. How have teachers individualized instruction for you?

3. Analyze your own style of learning and describe the best modes and methods teachers could adopt for your particular style.
4. What are the advantages and disadvantages of contingency contracts?
5. If a contingency contract fails to motivate adolescents, what might have gone wrong?
6. Write a weekly contract for adolescents in one course. Explain the rationale underlying the activities and grading scale.
7. What are five statements you have made about people's attitudes that are not stated in behavioral terminology? Reword them using behavioral statements.
8. How do you feel about the charge that rewarding students is "bribery?"
9   How do extrinsic and intrinsic rewards affect motivation?
10. With examples from your own life, explain how extrinsic rewards can be used to create intrinsic motivation.
11. What are the potential dangers of extrinsic rewards?
12. Describe three situations in which you are personally being motivated by extrinsic rewards and three others in which you are being motivated by intrinsic rewards. How do you feel about these situations?
13. How has flattery backfired in your life? How can you use compliments most effectively with adolescents?
14. When is praise most meaningful and motivating to you?
15. What are the advantages and disadvantages of norm-referenced grading?
16. In what ways have norm-referenced and criterion-referenced grading affected you, your friends, and adolescents in schools today?
17. How would you describe the leadership style of the teacher or supervisor whom you have most respected?
18. Which of your personal characteristics do you think will be advantageous and disadvantageous as a leader of adolescents?
19. What techniques can you suggest for helping adolescents feel comfortable in class discussions?
20. If you have ever led a group discussion, what errors did you make that detracted from its success?

"Here," said John to his father, "is my report card. And here," John added triumphantly, "is an old one of yours I found!"

chapter four

Improving adolescents' conduct

ADOLESCENT MISBEHAVIOR

Are contemporary youth pillaging and plundering their way through the nation's schools? Is misconduct in public schools beyond control? Are teenagers more delinquent or disruptive than their predecessors?

In the 1970s violence and vandalism in secondary schools were widely publicized, contributing to the assumption that delinquency is a recent and widespread phenomenon. In fact, violence and vandalism have been increasing gradually over several decades. From 1970 to 1973 the increases in homicides (up 18.5 percent), rapes (up 40 percent), robberies (up 36 percent), assaults (up 85 percent), and drug abuse (up 37 percent) are undeniable.[1] Vandalism alone costs somewhere from one hundred million to five hundred million dollars a year. The most costly delinquent crime is arson. But these acts are committed almost entirely in urban areas by a very small group of adolescents who repeatedly violate the law. Statistics do not show that American teenagers have become an unruly tribe of delinquents. In a 1976 nationwide poll only 4.3 percent of the teachers considered violence a major problem in school.[2]

Using statistics on violence and delinquency to suggest that contemporary youth are less disciplined or honorable than those of "the good old days" is problematic. To begin with, in 1900 only 11 percent of all adolescents attended high school. The rest were employed.[3] If the 89 percent who were working in 1900 had been in school, comparisons to contemporary youth might be more reliable. In addition, recording and classifying delinquent acts did not generally begin until the late 1960s, so our information about youngsters in previous generations is very limited. Even in 1980, data on delinquency were collected inconsistently, producing many conflicting statistics.[4]

Another statistical exaggeration is that most American secondary schools are dangerous. Undoubtedly some are. Most vandals, however, are not students who attend the school, and most conflict at school is not violent or directed against teachers.[5] Apparently misbehavior is influenced by a school's racial balance and geographical location. The risk of physical confrontation is greatest for those who are members of an urban school's minority group. Almost half of all attacks in urban schools are interracial and occur at the junior high school level.[6] The adolescent's sex also influences conduct and punishment (see Chapter 6). An important note, however, is that most delinquent youngsters are *not* disproportionately from lower socioeconomic or minority groups.[7]

One criticism levied against schools is that careful records have not been maintained to accurately identify juvenile offenders or their violations. Nevertheless, some generalizations about delinquents do seem justified by the available research.[8] Offenders often have histories of academic failure, learning disabilities, truancy, and low self-concepts. Males are more often delinquent and commit a greater variety of offenses than females, although female delinquency is increasing faster than that of males. There are almost no data, however, to show that teenagers commit proportionately more crimes than children or adults. The vast majority of adolescents are not troublemakers, driven by physiological or psychological forces that are unique to teenage years. One problem that is unique to adolescence, however, is suspension from school.

SCHOOL SUSPENSIONS

Are you aware that thousands of youngsters are excluded from school each day, mainly as punishment for smoking violations, tardiness, and truancy?[9] National studies have repeatedly shown that male students, especially black males, are suspended far more frequently than females.[10] In 1976, 1.8 million students were suspended from school, including

1.1 million whites and 0.5 million blacks.[11] Fewer than 120,000 of these suspended youngsters were referred to any alternative program to resolve their behavioral problems. Dramatic increases in suspensions of black students occurred after desegregation laws were enforced. Some contend that blacks are expelled for subjective or culturally biased infractions, such as disrespect, violations of dress codes, and noisiness. For example, teachers may mildly reprimand a white girl for "sassy" back talk, but physically punish a black boy for identical conduct because he is "aggressive and belligerent." If they are not literally kicked out, minority students may nevertheless be "pushed out" of school through repeated suspensions and punishments that result in academic deficits, lowered self-confidence, and negative feelings about education. Most young men and women are expelled for offenses that do not damage property or people: tardiness, truancy, smoking, and disrespect. Suspended students are usually in trouble for being uncooperative or belligerent, not for being violent or dangerous. Even brief suspensions from school may do irreparable academic or psychological damage to some adolescents. A three-day suspension can be the straw that breaks the camel's back—another high school dropout.

METHODS FOR IMPROVING ADOLESCENT CONDUCT

Unfortunately, less than half of the principals in a 1978 national survey had provided teachers with any in-service training on discipline or motivation, published the school's disciplinary regulations, tested students on school policies, or attempted behavior modification programs instead of suspension.[12] Despite the development of innovative options, many schools still cling to the old methods of disciplining students: contacting parents (86 percent of schools), referring students to counselors (73 percent), restricting privileges at school (48 percent), and using detention halls (46 percent).[13] Nonetheless, some educators have created successful programs that academically motivate and improve the conduct of youngsters.[14]

Cooling-Off Rooms

Angry or disruptive students leave class and receive counseling in the *cooling-off room*. This room is staffed with adult and peer counselors who help students design solutions to their problems before returning to the class where the conflict occurred.

Talk

Weekly individual and group counseling is arranged with a teacher for "high risk" junior high students. Students discuss their problems before major crises occur and receive advice all year from one teacher who knows them well.

Guided Group Interactions

Teachers identify school leaders and assign them randomly to heterogeneous groups. All students in the school are then placed in a group for peer counseling. For twelve weeks students mutually devise solutions to their problems. When a student's conduct in any area improves, he or she graduates from the group and receives a certificate.

Teacher Advocate

One teacher counsels regularly for several years with the same group of students and helps them resolve conflicts with their other teachers. The advantage of this counseling system is the continued rapport and camaraderie that develop over the years.

Alternative Schools

Evening or day programs exist for students who cannot function in traditional public schools. The common elements in these schools are individualized instruction, contingency contracting, and low student-teacher ratios.

Student Advocate

Teachers choose a council of thirty-six student leaders, including influential delinquents. When violations of school rules occur, the offenders each select an advocate from this council and the representatives develop a solution and punishment. Some delinquent leaders consequently become positive influences in the school by effectively resolving their peers' problems.

Schedule Changes

Discipline problems are recorded to determine how often and when they occur. Class periods are then rotated so that the same course does not always occupy the least or most desirable time of the day.

SOS—Save One Student

School personnel, including custodial and secretarial workers, choose one disruptive student to counsel and support throughout the year.

Buddy System

Two students create a team to assist each other in avoiding trouble and resolving problems. Guidance counselors can help arrange these teams and teach them the principles of behavior modification to assist each other.

Parent-Student Committees

A community group identifies the most frequent student offenses and devises disciplinary alternatives. The committee includes people from various socioeconomic and racial groups. Members of the school staff such as custodial and secretarial workers can add a special perspective on disciplinary methods.

Teacher Release Time

Teachers who are the least effective in motivating and managing their classes are released from teaching to accompany some of their most disruptive students throughout the day. This is an attempt to help these teachers see school from the student's perspective.

Principal's Round Table

The principal periodically selects ten students who represent the various populations in the school (not just the Honor Council and athletes). The students present their own ideas regarding the prevention of problems and appropriate punishment.

Detention Halls

Students are retained after school when they misbehave. Academic assignments must be completed during the detention period.

Smoking Clinic

Students who would otherwise be suspended for smoking are given the option of attending week-long evening seminars that discuss the hazards of smoking and methods of quitting. A parent must accompany the student. After four years of the smoking clinic, one school district reduced its suspensions for smoking violations from 45 percent to 13 percent.

Referral Forms

Before the principal punishes a student, the referring teacher must complete a form which specifies the remedies that have already been attempted: parent or student conference, after-school detention, consultation with counselor, a change in the student's classroom seat, or a report to the parents. This process encourages teachers to resolve conflicts by relying on their own resources, rather than by sending students away without attempting any resolutions.

Parent Phone Calls

Before any suspension, the principal or counselor phones the parents and discusses possible solutions. Conferences between the parents, the student, and a counselor can often be arranged to devise solutions.

Work Programs

Students who have earned demerits for misconduct in school work during weekends or after school on campus custodial projects.

Money in Escrow

The school board holds one dollar in escrow per student for the purpose of restoring damage to the school by vandals. Any money left at the year's end can be spent by students.

Minicourses

All students are required to take a minicourse about assaults, vandalism, and classroom management. The school's rules and the consequences of violations are also discussed. The hope is that adolescents will realize the serious impact of vandals' pranks on the victims and the taxpayers.

Phoning Parents

In the presence of the principal, the disruptive student has to telephone home to explain why he or she is in the principal's office. After the student has explained, the principal talks to the parent and they mutually decide upon an appropriate course of action.

Students' Handbooks

A handbook stating the school's policies is distributed to all students. This must be signed by the parents at the beginning of the school year to indicate that they, too, have read the material. The text is written at a fifth-grade reading level to insure comprehension by everyone.

Teacher Training

Teachers are given in-service training to provide them with techniques for motivating students academically, for discouraging inappropriate behavior, and for understanding cultural differences. With more skills in these areas, teachers can prevent many disciplinary problems from ever arising.

School Survival Training

In one particularly unique project, disruptive adolescents learn to use behavior modification for relating to their teachers. Students are trained to record their interactions with adults and to reinforce teachers with smiles, eye contact, attentive posture and verbal praise (see Chapter 11).

Faculty Seminars

Most faculties never get together formally to discuss disciplinary problems. But faculty meetings help dispel rumors about problems. In these meetings teachers help each other create specific plans for helping particular students or for remedying schoolwide problems. At the following meeting teachers report the results of each project and devise new techniques if necessary. Counselors and administrators should regularly share with the staff articles and ideas on preventive discipline and motivational teaching strategies.

Community Cards and Stroke Notes

The school gives students business cards that read: "You have just been served by _____, a student at Jefferson High School." When students perform a service for a fellow citizen, they leave a card with that person. Consequently, principals receive complimentary phone calls and letters from citizens and share these compliments with students. This technique establishes rapport between the community and the school and provides adolescents with ways to receive attention at school for their good conduct. "Stroke notes" follow this same principle. When teachers or administrators observe commendable conduct in school, they send a flattering note home to the adolescent's parents.

Photography Project

A few dozen of the most disruptive, unmotivated students are identified by teachers and are then photographed whenever they are studying. These photos are enlarged to poster size and hung in the main corridors. Contrary to expectations, when this was tried the posters were not destroyed and 75 percent of the misfits who were photographed improved their conduct in school. Apparently these adolescents felt that they had received peer and adult notoriety by "being caught being good."

Rumor Committee and Complaint Box

Junior high school students form a committee that prevents some of the school's problems from occurring by reporting rumors to school personnel about mounting pressures and individual conflicts. The committee becomes the mouthpiece for students who do not feel comfortable communicating directly with adults. A modification of this idea is to mount boxes in the corridors in which youngsters deposit their written complaints and suggestions. Although some crank notes are deposited, the majority of suggestions and tip-offs prevent disciplinary problems.

Conflict Management

In a survey of 8,500 adolescents, 91 percent felt that tension had not been reduced after they had supposedly "resolved" their conflicts with teachers or principals.[15] "Conflict management" is a way to help both parties feel more satisfied with resolutions. Each person candidly states his or her viewpoint but must only discuss observable behavior and may not allude to the other's personality or psychological analysis. For example, the student is allowed to say, "Ms. Jones made me furious when she called me stupid," but is not allowed to say, "Ms. Jones is a hateful human being." Likewise, the teacher can say, "Sam makes me mad when he curses at me in class," but is not allowed to say, "Sam has a disagreeable personality." Each person must then accurately rephrase the opponent's viewpoint. Once clear communication is achieved, the two people mutually design a behavioral remedy. A mediator sometimes helps by providing accurate restatements of each person's views and by suggesting solutions.

The In-School Suspension Center

Problems that cannot be remedied by any of the preceding suggestions might be resolved in an in-school suspension center.[16] When an in-school suspension center is created, unsupervised adolescents are kept off the streets, working parents are relieved of anxieties, and the school benefits financially from daily attendance compensation. Expelled students who would otherwise fall farther behind academically still receive instruction, while teachers can quickly isolate disruptive youngsters from their peers. The game of intentionally being expelled as a way of receiving a holiday is also undermined.

The initial step in creating a center is to explore the possibilities for federal funding. If no funds are available, adults already on the faculty can supervise the center by readjusting their schedules to provide the necessary free time for a staff. Two teachers can share this responsibility if their respective departments release them from half of their teaching duties. Ideally two adults should control the program—a certified teacher and a paraprofessional with talents in counseling and tutoring. These two people must not be coerced into the job and must not be seeking a reprieve from their classroom duties in search of an easier task.

Next, find a location for the center: an unused classroom, an extra teachers' lounge, a counseling room, or a mobile trailer. Equip the area with a dozen desks, storage cabinets, shelves with one copy of all the school's texts, a record player, a tape recorder, blank cassettes, headphones for private listening, bulletin boards, and a table large enough for board games. A telephone should be installed or a private line made available so that the staff can discuss problems during the day with parents who may work at night. Arrange some space for a student to sit who is disruptive, requires visual privacy to complete academic work, or needs private counseling. Several dozen paperback books and audiovisual kits on problems relevant to suspended students should also be available. Books and film strips are inexpensive, individualized ways to counsel adolescents with varied needs. Educational games should also be available for students who earn leisure time by fulfilling their academic and social contract.

When the academic year begins, explain the program to parents, teachers, and students. An essential message is that the center is not a "dumping ground," detention hall, or babysitting service. If the faculty relies on it for these purposes, the project will become a way of discouraging adults from developing their own skills for managing and motivating students. Emphasize the punitive aspects of the program: segregation from peers, constant supervision, loss of recess, parental disapproval, and confinement all day to a single room. The faculty's and students' questions, reservations, and recommendations should be thoroughly discussed. Progress reports from the center should be shared with every member of the school, including bus drivers and custodial and cafeteria workers. Everyone's input is solicited.

Administrators sometimes abuse the in-school suspension center by sending students there whose problems do not warrant expulsion. To lessen the possibility of such abuses and to gather accurate information about the school's disciplinary problems, the suspension center's staff should record the sex, race, incident, and length of assignment for all suspended students. These data should be shared regularly with a faculty-parent disciplinary committee.

When a youngster is sent to the principal's office for an infraction, he or she should not be sent to the suspension center until the following day. This provides time for the case to be explained to the suspension center staff and for students to ask their teachers to send their academic assignments to the center for the designated days. A critical factor in successful suspension centers is that academic work continues. Teachers must send lessons before each day's classes begin, so that students can complete their work each morning in the suspension center. No academic penalties are levied against students if they complete their lessons. Punishing students by deducting academic credit usually only increases their hostility and decreases their motivation. If students' offenses are too serious to allow them to return to regular classes before their assignment to the center, guidance counselors can intervene. Drunkenness or violence probably warrant immediate isolation, whereas tardiness or disrespect do not. If the center is filled to capacity (fifteen students for two adults), the principal may delay the assignment a few days until there is a vacancy.

The school's regulations and penalties should be distributed to parents and students when the year begins (Table 7). This publication is designed to prevent students from feeling discriminated against and to mollify angry parents who might claim that their child was not aware of the consequences of his or her actions. Some people may protest that establishing guidelines is too difficult because everyone's offense is unique and the punishment, therefore, should vary. The counterargument is that inconsistent punishment creates hostility.

Which counseling strategies are appropriate when some students are in the center for ten days and others stay only a few? Most programs have discovered that behavioral approaches such as reality therapy and self-

TABLE 7. Publicized Disciplinary Code

Offense	In-school Suspension Center
Cutting one class	= 2 days
Cutting one day	= 4 days
Fighting	= 8 days
Disrespect to teacher	= 5 days
Six tardies	= 3 days
Smoking in restricted areas	= 3 days
Alcohol or drugs on campus	= 5 days
Stealing	= 5 days
Possession of weapon	= 10 days out of school suspension
Second offense	= double time

modification are most effective and adaptable. Other programs obtain desirable results with values clarification, peer counseling, and transactional analysis. The choice of methods should depend on the student's ability to accept personal responsibility for his or her actions, since willingness to assign blame fairly varies greatly among adolescents.

Attracted by the individual tutoring, counseling, contracting, and complimentary notes to their parents, some suspended students do not want to leave the suspension center. These students need further counseling to devise specific remedies for the problems that make them seek refuge in the center. All in all, in-school suspension centers are tremendously successful in improving adolescents' conduct by counseling and by keeping youngsters off the streets.

METHODS TO DISCOURAGE TRUANCY

The image of barefooted youth "playing hooky" and entertaining themselves on the shady banks of a cool river is part of American folklore. Less romantically, however, truancy in high schools has reached epidemic proportions. Almost two million students are regularly truant from school each year, with large urban areas being the most severely affected. In Boston, for example, truancy doubled to 25 percent of the school population from 1974 to 1979.[17] In one survey 75 percent of the urban school districts stated that tardiness and truancy were the main reasons for disciplinary action.[18]

Although school phobia may generally be associated with elementary school children, some psychologists suggest that truancy is one way adolescents manifest their fear of school.[19] While young children fear separation from their parents, adolescents fear the unpleasant experiences they have learned to expect at school. Fear of failure, peer rejection, or conflict with teachers all contribute to adolescents' school phobia. Rather than crying or openly admitting fear, some adolescents simply elect to avoid unpleasant situations through truancy.

What can we do to alleviate this situation? To begin with, we can reward attendance with points added to grades or exclusion from certain tests. Replicating college systems, some public schools permit a predesignated number of absences from each class, after which the student is automatically dropped from the course. In a similar approach there are no excused or unexcused absences, but after the tenth absence the student loses credit for the course and chooses one of two options: remain in class without course credit or withdraw entirely to a study hall. Two tardies are counted as one absence. Although some opponents might argue that this plan is too harsh, advocates contend that only when truants experience serious consequences will they decide to attend school.[20]

In one high school truants received fifty cents for attending a meeting at which the principal explained a contingency contract for truancy but refrained from any lectures about the virtues of attending school.[21] Students then wrote a contract with a teacher's assistance specifying that they would receive a ticket for each class attended. Bonus tickets were awarded for consecutive days of attendance, and teachers regularly complimented students for their attendance. At the end of three weeks, all tickets were entered in a raffle for prizes. Of course the more tickets a person had earned the greater his or her chance of winning. At the end of eight weeks the program ended and teachers discussed with the students the social consequences of attendance—no nagging from adults and freedom from the anxieties of getting caught. The program succeeded in reducing truancy, lowering suspensions, and pleasing the students.

A clever variation of this contracting approach included a pool hall proprietor, a grandmother, girlfriends, and parents.[22] These people agreed to be the mediators in helping truants write attendance contracts with a school counselor. The rewards for attendance varied in accordance with each truant's own wishes: playing pool, being with a girlfriend, earning money, or receiving weekend privileges at home. The counselor telephoned the mediators periodically for progress reports. Even when the counselor was absent for two weeks, the truants maintained their school attendance. If girlfirends and pool hall proprietors fail, how about a friend at school? In the "buddy system," a truant and a friend who regularly attends school sign a mutual contract. The points earned by each for attendance are combined, and rewards are based on their team total.

Of course there are more aversive ways to reduce truancy.[23] One school district gathered all the truants together in court early in the school year for a lecture on the legalities involved. Fines could also be levied against parents, and probation could be invoked against foster parents. Truants can also be assigned to special schools with individualized instruction and frequent reinforcement.

The telephone is sometimes a valuable resource.[24] Members of the

PTA telephone parents each day that their child is absent to discuss causes, consequences, and remedies. Rather than having a stranger telephone, an adult who communicates well with the student can make the contact. Not surprisingly, given some truants' unhappiness and loneliness at school, the representative who calls parents in some cases may be the custodian. Some schools also provide a wake-up call for youngsters whose parents work early shifts. Truancy fundamentally indicates that secondary schools are not very appealing places from the adolescent's perspective. But until a provocative curriculum and teachers attract adolescents, we can use other incentives to encourage attendance.

CORPORAL PUNISHMENT

Inflicting physical pain on adolescents as a way of controlling their conduct is condemned by the National Education Association, the National Center for Corporal Punishment, the American Psychological Association, the Commission on the Reform of Secondary Education, and the American Friends Peace Committee.[25] Many teachers (46 percent) also oppose corporal punishment.[26] Then why does the practice of hitting adolescents at school continue? One hypothesis is that teachers and principals who hit students receive a shortlived form of reinforcement. Most students behave more appropriately immediately following physical punishment. The irony is that after physical punishment the misbehavior usually becomes more frequent and more serious.[27] Adults may also hit students because they are unaware of other remedies. Consequently, more training for educators in classroom management, motivation, and communication might result in less corporal punishment.

Corporal punishment causes some youngsters to engage in escape mechanisms such as truancy and dropping out of school. Others become hostile or withdrawn. Striking students often preempts any further communication and conveys the idea that inflicting physical pain on others is acceptable. Several states have outlawed corporal punishment with no resulting loss of control when other disciplinary methods are employed.[28] The National Commission on the Reform of Secondary Education recommends that hitting adolescents be abolished as "cruel and unusual punishment." The "Spare the rod and spoil the child" philosophy, is in dire need of revision.

CONTINGENCY MANAGEMENT

Many of the suggestions for improving adolescents' conduct at home or at school rely on the principles of contingency management.[29] These methods are sometimes referred to as *behavioral psychology, operant psychology,* or *behavioral modification.* By whatever name, the methods work! A contingency contract is a popular, expedient, and fruitful method for immediately improving most adolescents' behavior. Some schools modify the concept of a written contract by rewarding students' good behavior with recreation room privileges, leisure time, or raffles with prizes from the community's merchants. One high school which was plagued with disciplinary problems established a school "bank." Students earned points for academic and social conduct. They then deposited the points into their bank acount. The points earned interest in the account and could be withdrawn at any time and cashed in for a variety of special privileges. Contracts that involve the adolescent's family are often the most effective.

The methods of contingency management, however, do not always have to be as elaborate as written contracts or school banking services. Verbal praise, complimentary notes to parents, good grades, or a few extra minutes of leisure time at the end of class are all powerful incentives for adolescents to behave well. Adults must work more diligently to "catch kids being good," rather than only punishing inappropriate conduct. One school, for instance, discovered that piping music into the cafeteria during lunch caused students to keep tables clean and behave courteously. Whenever messiness or loudness became a problem, the music was stopped for several days. Another school rewarded adolescents for keeping their campus clean by arranging for the local newspaper to write a feature article on the youngsters' efforts. An adult who concentrates on using rewards correctly can maintain most adolescents' good behavior without resorting to punishment or threats.

In using contingency management, we must follow the procedures carefully and consistently. First, state the expectations to an adolescent in behavioral terms (Tables 4 and 5). Gather data by sampling the youngster's baseline performance and set behavioral goals only *slightly* beyond the present level. Discuss the goal and the rewards with the adolescent, then consistenly, frequently, and immediately reinforce all initial improvements. Remember that shaping new behavior requires reinforcing successive approximations of the ultimate goal. Administer the reinforcement after, not before, the adolescent improves: "I will give you five minutes free at the end of class if you do not curse at anyone during the hour," rather than "If I give you five minutes to talk to your friends, you must promise that you won't swear for the rest of the period." To prevent satiation from occurring, vary the rewards or allow students to choose their own reinforcement by cashing in *tokens*. For instance, a student who earns ten points may choose any activity from a reinforcement list.

In some situations adolescents will only improve their conduct when there are penalties for bad behavior in addition to rewards for good conduct. Two effective ways to combine rewards and punishment are by extinction and response-cost. *Extinction* means ignoring bad conduct by withholding all attention until the person behaves appropriately. Most teachers yell, threaten, talk with, or offer assistance to the disruptive student. But when the same student is well behaved, teachers usually pay no attention. The net result is that most adults are reinforcing adolescents for being disruptive and ignoring them for being cooperative. The immediate result of extinction is that the youngster's behavior will worsen because he or she is testing the adult's limits. But eventually, if absolutely no attention or reinforcement follows, the bad conduct will cease. One of the disadvantages in using extinction is that the adult must have an enormous amount of control and patience in order to completely ignore all annoying conduct. Another disadvantage is that the adolescent's conduct may be harmful to others and cannot be allowed to disappear slowly. Extinction is most wisely used for eliminating annoying habits or conduct that is harmless to others. For instance, a youngster who constantly interrupts a teacher by blurting out jokes can be ignored when interrupting and praised at the end of class for refraining.

Response-cost is a more reliable, less taxing method for punishing poor conduct. As the term implies, adolescents' inappropriate responses will "cost" them a reward. An example is the coach who rewards all students who arrive at practice promptly and in proper attire by reducing their daily laps, but who makes all tardy or improperly dressed players run three extra laps. Response-cost allows adolescents a fair chance to avoid any unpleasant consequences and to earn rewards regularly.

By using contingency management strategies, adults give adolescents the prerequisites for learning self-management methods (see Chapter 11). Unfortunately, most adults do not assess adolescents' misconduct from the perspective of contingency management. We inadvertently reinforce bad behavior while ignoring the good. For instance, a student who tells the truth about cheating, stealing, or breaking a rule is invariably punished for his or her candor. But being dishonest yields rewards such as higher grades from cheating or material possessions from stealing. Adults who want to change an adolescent's conduct will have to offer an attractive incentive. A student could occasionally be given a reprieve from punishment for being honest. Adolescents who turn in lost items could be told that if the owner is not found in a week, they will be given the goods. Students who admit that they are unprepared for a test could be given an extra day to study with a few points deducted rather than feeling that they have to cheat on the exam. Wise adults study an adolescent's misbehavior by identifying the payoffs that are maintaining the conduct, such as peer attention, higher grades, or escaping a penalty at home.

ACADEMICS AND MISBEHAVIOR

Despite all the alternatives for improving adolescents' social conduct, the most potent medicine is prevention. Disruptive youngsters are almost always frustrated by academic problems. When adolescents succeed academically and are enthusiastic about their courses, inappropriate behavior diminishes. Concentrating too much effort on ways to discipline students often diverts our energy from creative teaching. A more relevant curriculum and more motivating classroom activities are probably the most powerful weapons against poor conduct. Teachers whose classes are stimulating, friendly, and well organized are not often besieged by discipline problems. Even adolescents who consistently misbehave at school are often self-disciplined and motivated in exciting classes where they can achieve self-esteem through academic success. Although teachers often blame parents and society's low standards for discipline problems at school, adolescents blame a dull curriculum, poor communication with teachers, and lack of involvement with the school's goals and activities.[30] When adolescents perceive school as a friendly, exciting place that enhances their self-esteem, they do not destroy, deface, or disrupt.

Questions for Discussion and Review

1. How could you refute the assertion, "Teenagers today are a bunch of delinquents"?
2. In what ways might racism and sexism influence who is expelled from school?
3. Which of the alternatives to suspension discussed in this chapter do you like least? Why?
4. How can you include parents in resolving adolescents' disciplinary problems?
5. On what grounds are in-school suspension centers justified?
6. In addition to this chapter's ideas, what alternatives can you offer for controlling or preventing misbehavior in secondary schools?
7. In what situations do you believe out-of-school suspensions are warranted?
8. What conduct do you consider unacceptable for adolescents at school? What punishment would you arrange for these violations?
9. What changes in a secondary school's curriculum, faculty, or regulations might decrease adolescents' misbehavior?
10. What are the components of a successful in-school suspension center?
11. What arguments might some critics levy against in-school suspension centers and how would you respond?
12. When you were an adolescent, how did you and your classmates misbehave? How would you recommend preventing or punishing this conduct?
13. What are some persuasive arguments for and against corporal punishment? What's your view?
14. How would you design a contract for an in-school suspension center?
15. What would you recommend for a school whose students are suspended mainly for truancy and smoking violations?
16. What remedies are available for the kinds of adolescent misbehavior that frighten you most?
17. How could a new definition of masculinity improve some adolescents' conduct?
18. How could you dissuade another adult from using corporal punishment to improve adolescents' behavior?
19. For each of the following situations, explain why the adult's plan or conduct is inappropriate. Keep in mind the criteria for successful contingency management projects. What would you recommend that each of these adults try next?

Donald is a very bright student who almost always volunteers creative and correct answers in class discussions. Unfortunately, he constantly blurts out answers before anyone else has a chance to participate. Many students are becoming bored or frustrated because Donald's answers prevent them from speaking. Mr. Rodriguez announces that everyone must first raise a hand and wait to be called on before answering. The next day Donald shouts out another answer. Mr. Rodriguez compliments him and says, "Next time please raise your hand." After a few weeks Mr. Rodriguez abandons his rule about hand raising because Donald is still dominating the class and nobody else ever volunteers an answer.

Leroy is a daydreamer who is failing math and talking to other students in class while they try to work. He is a capable student who could do the work if he chose. Whenever Leroy bothers others or daydreams, Ms. Williams approaches him and either offers to help, gives him a peptalk, or reprimands him for pestering his friends. Although she promises Leroy a passing grade if he will work, he continues to ignore his math assignments in class. Ms. Williams concludes in exasperation that "this behavior modification business is for the birds!"

By using time-out and extinction, Mr. Litcher has improved most students' conduct in his math class. But two very talkative students, Sam and Leon, still interrupt the class frequently and old George continues to come to class late. Mr. Litcher announces to these three students, "From now on any time you do anything wrong, you'll be punished for it." The three boys responded very belligerently.

Samantha is the class clown. Almost daily she creates uproarious laughter in the middle of the lesson with her antics and witty comments. Even the teacher laughs. But Samantha's wit is causing many classmates to lose their academic concentration and is making the lessons very disorganized. Ms. Kaufman tried punishment by sending Samantha to the office and tried extinction by not laughing at Samantha's remarks. Both methods failed. Finally she tried sending Samantha to a special seat in the back of the class every time she interrupted the lesson with her humor. This approach seems to have made matters even worse.

Mr. Polito decides to reward his history class for completing their homework since so few students ever turn in an assignment. He carefully explains that everyone will receive one point for every completed assignment and that whoever has twenty points at the end of the six weeks can have one free class period. Very few students, however, begin turning in homework.

Ms. Snodgrass has just begun teaching a seventh-grade vocational education class. Because there is so much potentially dangerous equipment in the room, she is worried about her students' safety. Her fourth-period class is very rowdy. Almost everyone runs, throws things, and shoves other classmates against tables or equipment. There is so little appropriate conduct that Ms. Snodgrass really cannot try rewards as a way to improve conduct. She cannot use time out because all thirty students would have to be sent away. Ignoring inappropriate conduct is not an option, since the students' physical safety is too serious a danger to allow the slow process of extinction to work. Ms. Snodgrass is baffled and desperate for a solution.

part two

THE IMPACT OF PHYSICAL NEEDS AND SEX ROLES ON MOTIVATION

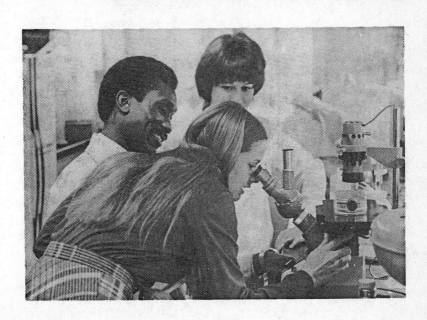

chapter five

Using physiology to help adolescents

THE RELEVANCE OF BIOLOGICAL DATA

Adolescent psychology texts traditionally devote an entire chapter to physical development. Three candid contemporary books on anatomy and sexuality are *Our Bodies, Ourselves; Changing Bodies, Changing Selves; and Men's Bodies, Men's Selves.*[1] Adults need to know physiological facts in order to answer adolescents' questions accurately and completely. Besieged by myths about conception, contraception, and the physical abilities of males and females, adolescents need unabashed, unbiased responses. Adults who are unwilling to provide sexual information can at least furnish youngsters with relevant books on anatomy and sexuality. But beyond our ability to disseminate sexual information to adolescents, what is the value of biological data? How do biological concerns relate to adolescents' personalities or academic achievement?

NUTRITION AND BEHAVIOR

One relevant biological fact is that some adolescents literally lack "food for thought." Food's influence on behavior has even led some people to the erroneous conclusion that certain ethnic groups are genetically programmed to be lazy and lethargic.[2] In fact, most minority groups are so poorly nourished that their improper diet, not genes, interferes with their academic or vocational performance. Hispanic migrant workers and Indians are the most malnourished Americans. Poorly fed adolescents, however, may not necessarily look emaciated. Some of the most overweight youngsters live on the least well-balanced diets. In deciding whether an adolescent's academic problems are related to nutrition, we must identify the kinds of foods he or she eats and not just the amount.

Food can affect adolescents' academic motivation and social conduct.[3] A common disorder is "the sugar blues." Adolescents who eat a lot of sugared foods such as cake, candy, and cereals will experience an immediate surge of energy followed by a dramatic loss of power. Drowsiness or a midmorning slump results from eating heavily sugared foods for breakfast. The student may be very energetic following breakfast but will begin to crave another sweet treat when the blood's sugar level plummets at midmorning. Excessive sugar can also interfere with academic concentration by creating restlessness from too much initial sugar and listlessness or irritability when the sugar supply is depleted. A breakfast or lunch that contains proteins and carbohydrates rather than sugar will provide an evenly distributed supply of energy throughout the day. Vitamin deficiences are also related to forgetfulness, lethargy, depression, nervousness, irritability, and mental confusion. When discussing academic or social problems with adolescents, we should always consider food as an important factor that may be influencing their mood and behavior.

AIR POLLUTION AND ACHIEVEMENT

Going out for a bit of fresh air might also help some youngsters academically.[4] Air trapped inside buildings accumulates toxic pollutants which sometimes cause forgetfulness, sleepiness, headaches, and apathy, especially during winter when everyone huddles indoors at lunch and recess. Leaky old buildings allow enough outside air to penetrate so that fresh air continually circulates, but modern, well-insulated schools prevent this natural ventilation. Some evidence suggests that the proportion of negative and positive ions in the air also influences irritability and depression in certain "weather-sensitive" people. Certain winds increase the number of positive ions and may aggravate people, encouraging aggressive conduct.[5] Like these "devil winds," stale air inside schools contains an excess of positive ions. Solution? We can open the windows in our class-rooms and encourage adolescents to step outside during the day for a breath of fresh air.

Unfortunately the outside air can also be an academic hazard. Like the paint in old tenements, automobile exhaust fumes contain lead, which sometimes impairs a student's hand-eye coordination and reasoning abil-ities.[6] Inner city schools are afflicted more than suburban schools because of their constant exposure to traffic. Males are more sensitive to lead poisoning than females. Consequently, pills that lower the lead content in the body have improved the conduct of some hyperactive boys.

SMOKING AND SCHOOL

An adolescent's decision to smoke cigarettes sometimes has academic ramifications. Especially in junior high schools, smoking is often prohib-ited. Many youngsters are eventually suspended from school for repeat-edly violating the no-smoking policy. Deprived of academic instruction, suspended students jeopardize more than their physical health.

With the availability of modern techniques for combatting the nic-otine habit, schools should be able to abandon the policy of suspending students for smoking violations. If smoking must be a punishable offense, we can assign juvenile offenders to a smoking clinic. Violators must attend the clinic for one week, accompanied by a parent. Medical authorities show films and lead discussions about physical damage from nicotine. Psychologists then present methods of self-control to stop smoking. One school district reduced suspensions 45 percent by instituting smoking clinics.[7] Rather than lecturing about cancer, some campaigns appeal to the smoker's sexual vanity and the desire for social approval. Smoking causes bad breath, disgusting coughs, yellow teeth, stained fingers, smelly clothes, and premature wrinkling of the skin. Some evidence also suggests that smoking interferes with academic and athletic performance by lower-ing the blood's oxygen supply, which is necessary for physical and mental alertness. Since athletic excellence is a basis for many male adolescents' social status and self-esteem, they may be more likely to abandon the habit for immediate athletic gains than for the delayed reward of good health.

PHYSICAL APPEARANCE AND MOTIVATION

How does physical appearance influence adolescent motivation? Unfortunately, we sometimes unconsciously attribute social and mental traits to youngsters on the basis of their physical characteristics.[8] Adults often assume that attractive adolescents are intelligent, popular, studious, and well cared for at home. Fat youngsters, on the other hand, often conjure up an image of being slovenly, undisciplined, dependent, and lazy. Adolescents with physical problems such as bad teeth or dirtiness generally repel more adults than youngsters whose unappealing characteristics are beyond their control, such as those with scars from burns. Our expectations about adolescents' social, athletic, and academic performance may contribute to self-fulfilling prophecies. Sexism and racism are the most striking examples of how physical appearance alters our interactions and creates sulf-fulfilling prophecies for adolescents. Two physical traits—skin color and reproductive organs—cause many adults to form immediate impressions of an adolescent's personality and potential. We will only be able to motivate youngsters on the basis of their unique needs if we learn to ignore the physical characteristics of color, sex, body type, and beauty when we relate to them.

An adolescent's self-confidence is also partially dependent on physical traits. Being called "tubby," "skinny," or "cute" affects self-esteem for almost everyone. If an adolescent's body and facial features differ considerably from the dominant culture's ever-changing definition of "beauty," he or she may feel frustrated and dissatisfied. One decade's hero has the body of Charles Atlas, and the next decade's hero has the build of a marathon runner. Adolescents who are not Caucasians may be more adversely affected by the culture's arbitrary definitions of beauty than their Anglo classmates. "Black is beautiful" is a concept that developed during the 1960s and that helped to counteract the narrow standard of beauty in effect then. But some adolescents may still feel frustrated and dissatisfied since most presentations of attractiveness in textbooks and in the media are from a Caucasian perspective.

The speed at which an adolescent's body matures might also affect self-esteem and conduct for some individuals. Boys who mature slowly are often judged less attractive and less "masculine" than their more quickly maturing peers. Feeling unmanly, small boys sometimes decide to attract attention through aggression, classroom antics, or delinquent activities.

Girls who mature slowly have fewer difficulties than boys but may still feel a need to gain peer approval to compensate for their slow physical development. Both male and female adolescents who mature quickly may share one similar disadvantage: Adults often expect physically advanced adolescents to behave more maturely than their age and experience warrant. Most adolescents, however, are content with their bodies and are not permanently or dramatically affected by early or late maturation.[9]

Because facial features, the body's shape, and the speed of maturation may affect an adolescent's motivation, we cannot ignore their impact on academic and social conduct. Helping adolescents feel more satisfied with themselves physically might help them academically and socially. We can begin by encouraging youngsters to expand their definitions of beauty. Through pictures and literature we can introduce bodies and faces that are beautiful in many shapes, sizes, and colors. Through reading and discussions, we can reinforce the idea that each culture defines attractiveness in a distinct and arbitrary way. By discussing the wide range of human weights and heights, we also help adolescents understand that most bodies do not resemble movie stars or sports heroes. If we help youngsters feel more satisfied with their faces and bodies, perhaps some of the shyness or aggressiveness of those who feel physically ashamed will disappear.

PHYSICALLY HANDICAPPED ADOLESCENTS

The youngsters whose motivation suffers most from judgments based on physical appearance are the physically handicapped.[10] Even though adolescents with physical disabilities are not stupid or graceless, many of us respond to them as though they were mentally retarded or slow learners. Like racial minorities, most handicapped Americans are victims of unfounded myths and overt prejudice. For instance, although a law in 1968 required that federally financed buildings be accessible to physically impaired citizens, fewer than 10 percent had complied by 1974. It was not until 1975 that the Act for the Education of Handicapped Children prevented public schools from excluding the physically impaired. Rather than viewing a physical handicap as just one aspect of the individual's whole personality, most of us overlook the normal behavior and talents of handicapped adolescents. We ourselves forget and we fail to teach kids that President Roosevelt with polio, President Kennedy with Addison's disease,

Alexander the Great and Caesar with epilepsy, Lord Byron with a clubfoot, Beethoven and Edison with their deafness, and John Milton with no sight were all "handicapped" people. By perceiving physically impaired adolescents as members of an oppressed minority group rather than as deviants, we might begin to improve our conduct towards them.

Educators should include parents of the handicapped in every important discussion about their child's educational or vocational program. Parents must be accorded the right to question educational practices and to insist on specific answers to disturbing situations. In particular, parents from lower socioeconomic or minority groups must be treated with equal respect in discussions with professionals. Schools can even sponsor workshops to train the least educated parents to communicate assertively with educators and counselors. Although they may claim to have no prejudices toward the handicapped, many grownups unconsciously respond less favorably toward permanently disabled youngsters (amputees) than toward the temporarily disabled (broken arm). Colleges and public schools, therefore, should be providing adults with more information about and experience with physically impaired adolescents.

Another way of motivating handicapped adolescents is to teach other youngsters about physical disabilities through the high school's curriculum. One series of high school classroom exercises and materials gives examples of handicapped people's contributions to American society.[11] Books and television programs that portray the strengths of physically handicapped people could help everyone feel more at ease relating to handicapped adolescents. Schools should also provide handicapped peer tutors and paraprofessionals who work with all adolescents as role models. By including handicapped kids in classes with physically normal peers and by encouraging them to expand their future vocational options, schools can replace pity with personal pride and power.

SPORTS AND MOTIVATION

Sports and Adolescent Boys

Adolescent athletes are not necessarily an advantaged group. Believing that fame and fortune depend on their athletic skills, many adolescents are unmotivated to prepare themselves for any future vocation other than sports. Some adults inadvertently contribute to adolescent boys' visions of athletic grandeur and discourage social and academic development in male athletes. Although they admonish athletes who fail academically, some teachers nevertheless lower their academic standards or make other concessions for athletes. There are occasional stories of teachers who are pressured by administrators and coaches into making "special arrangements" to insure that athletes will not fail academically and be disqualified from playing. Adults who support athletes' accomplishments while ignoring scholars' feats are undermining academic motivation.

Despite popular myths that sports "build character," the research shows a different picture.[12] Unquestioning obedience to authority and a disregard for injury and suffering are two unfortunate values many athletes learn. Critics of America's obsession with sports also point out that athletes are taught to value violence, to base their self-esteem only on winning, and to experience excessive anxiety over being "masculine" at all times. Nonathletic boys often suffer from an inferiority complex around the "jocks." Team players may even develop jealousies and feel inferior if they are not one of the superstars. Although adolescent athletes learn how to compete, cooperate, and discipline themselves, the obsession with athletics often decreases boys' motivation to develop skills in personal relationships and academics. The alternative is not to abandon sports but to encourage more noncompetitive games. Adolescents can also learn to develop many different physical skills, rather than specializing in one event to become a superstar. Sports should supplement, not replace, an adolescent's social, academic, and personal development.

Sports and Adolescent Girls

While the boys score points, the girls cheer.[13] The social and academic benefits of sports are almost exclusively reserved for males. The National Federation of High School Athletic Associations says that contrary to popular belief, girls' participation in sports has declined since the passage of Title IX, which guaranteed sexual equity.[14] Perhaps this decline is related to the fact that most schools continue to deprive female adolescents of the same athletic encouragement and opportunities as males. Girls' coaches are usually paid less, accorded secondary status in access to facilities and scheduling games, and given small budgets. Unfortunately, athletic inequity denies female adolescents certain academic privileges as well. Athletic scholarships that enable adolescents to pursue college degrees have traditionally been for boys only, which especially penalizes girls from poor families. Some male athletes also profit academically when their school provides tutoring for players and when coaches supervise their teams' educational development. Sports also gives many young men the self-confidence, assertiveness, competitiveness, and organizational skills that aid them in future careers. There is even some evidence that sports foster mathematical skills.[15]

Why are so few girls motivated to participate in sports? Aside from the inequities in money, coaching, and facilities, girls and the adults who guide them often believe that sweat, muscles, and vigorous physical activity are unfeminine.[16] To discourage girls from participating in vigorous sports adults often warn them about ugly muscles, homosexuality among athletes, and dangers to their reproductive organs. Some adults also discourage girls from exercise during menstruation and pregnancy. If all else fails, grownups can frighten girls with stories about ugly scars, bruises, or broken bones that might result from sports. Most adolescents do not learn that physical exercise during menstruation and pregnancy is healthy, that their sexual organs are far more protected from injury than boys', and that females win Olympic medals during every phase of the monthly cycle. Furthermore, bulky muscles come from testosterone (the male hormone), not from excessive exercise.

If girls are to benefit academically and physically from sports, we must correct their misunderstandings about their anatomy and their physical potential. With role models, duscussions, and books, we can encourage girls to get out of the bleachers and cheerleading squads and onto the courts, fields, and tracks.

Sports as Academic Therapy

Although too much emphasis on sports can detract from academic motivation, physical exercise usually enhances mental accomplishments. Rigorous physical exercise such as jogging, swimming, or biking often reduces anxiety and increases self-confidence in the classroom.[17] "Exertion therapy" improves academic skills by giving the adolescent more physical energy for classroom concentration as well as the self-esteem and self-discipline that develop from mastering a physical skill. Along with learning methods for self-control, adolescents who are academically or socially troubled should be encouraged to exercise strenuously for at least thirty minutes a day. Some counselors and teachers even join troubled kids after school to jog together. The activity creates a unique opportunity for camaraderie that is seldom possible in the classroom. Hostile or shy youngsters may learn to communicate with adults in classroom situations as well as on the track. Exercising together generally draws people closer together as friends.

Another way that sports can benefit adolescents academically is through the coach-player relationship. Recognizing their power to influence athletes academically, some coaches conscientiously oversee each player's educational progress. Physical education departments sometimes arrange tutoring for players with academic problems and counseling for those without the self-discipline to study. Students who disregard other adults' advice often heed their coach's warnings or counsel. There is some evidence that coaches are especially influential with boys from poor families.[18] In some schools physical education teachers agree to encourage students to read by displaying paperback books about sports in the gym and by recommending specific books to the poorest readers. Other coaches may require weekly academic reports from each athlete's teachers.

PREGNANCY AND MOTIVATION

Each year in America almost eleven million teenaged girls become pregnant and nearly 600,000 have their babies. During 1976 only about one-third of the sexually active adolescents regularly used contraceptives. One-fourth never used contraceptives and 40 percent used them occasionally. By the age of nineteen, nearly 70 percent of all girls have had intercourse, yet only 40 percent in a 1977 survey even knew which days of a monthly cycle were riskiest for conception. Only 20 percent of adolescent mothers complete high school. To compound these sad statistics, adolescent pregnancies cost taxpayers about 8.3 billion dollars yearly in welfare and related outlays.[19]

Why aren't adolescents more motivated to prevent pregnancy? Most adolescents still do not receive adequate information about their sexual selves.[20] There are virtually no advertising campaigns or programs advocating the responsible use of contraceptives. Some communities try to compensate for the lack of sexual information given to adolescents in school or at home by having famous athletes and performers endorse contraceptives on the radio. The impact of the existing sex education classes in school is also significant. Clases in sex education reduce venereal disease, pregnancy, and intolerance for others' sexual conduct. Contrary to some adults' fears, sex education does not often increase adolescents' sexual activity or alter their personal sexual values.[21] Although accidental pregnancy is not the only reason why adolescent girls quit school, motherhood is seldom an academic incentive. Not until the early 1970s did national policy forbid schools to deprive pregnant adolescents of an education. Nowadays most metropolitan schools accommodate pregnant students' needs with flexible class schedules, evening courses, homebound teachers, child care services, and economic resources. Many smaller, rural schools, however, still make unmarried mothers feel uncomfortable and unwelcomed.

As far as educators are concerned, the primary way to prevent pregnancy from interfering with academic achievement is to educate adolescents beforehand about their own bodies. In addition to the essential facts about conception and contraception adolescents need information about the financial, psychological, and academic consequences of parenthood. The impact of sex education and easy access to contraceptives remains to be seen. Hopefully, many adolescent girls can eventually be spared the emotional and educational stress of unwelcomed pregnancy.

The adolescent father is traditionally excluded from research on unwanted pregnancies. The consequences of teenage pregnancies on young men are not very clear. Some planned parenthood associations, however, are realizing the unfairness of placing all the responsibility for birth control on girls. Some advertisements are consequently being aimed at young men. Counseling adolescent fathers is also becoming more popular. The most comprehensive study of adolescent fathers does not support the myth that boys exploit or trick girls into a sexual relationship.[22] The unwed mothers and fathers in Pannor's study were not disproportionately from poor families and did not have a pattern of repeated illegitimate pregnancies. The adolescent fathers often felt guiltier about the pregnancy than the unwed mothers and expressed concern over the child's future. The researchers suggested that teenagers would be more motivated to use contraceptives if more boys were included in programs about contraception and the responsibilities of parenthood.

Questions for Discussion and Review

1. How can biological factors affect academic motivation?
2. To determine whether diet and physical fitness were influencing an adolescent's conduct, what questions would you ask the youngster?
3. How can smoking interfere with motivation and what can adults do to help adolescent nicotine addicts?
4. How can physical appearance affect an adolescent's personality?
5. What are your feelings around physically handicapped people and how might these feelings affect your ability to motivate handicapped youth?
6. What classroom activities or changes in the curriculum could improve a handicapped adolescent's motivation?
7. What would help you overcome your personal uneasiness around handicapped people?
8. How can sports favorably or adversely affect adolescents' academic motivation?
9. How could you persuade parents that their daughter would benefit from participation in sports?
10 What special advice would you give to adolescent athletes?
11. Specifically how would you encourage adolescent participation in sports without causing interference with academic motivation?
12. What specific change can schools make to insure that biological factors are working for, rather than against, adolescent achievement and motivation?

With furrowed brow the coach studied the report card intently. "Well, it says you got one D and four F's. Looks to me, Moose, like you been putting too much time in on one subject."

chapter six

Creating a nonsexist environment for adolescents

NONSEXIST EDUCATION: TEMPEST IN A TEAPOT?

Most educators and counselors have finally agreed that racial discrimination must end and should rightfully be illegal. Yet ironically some adults who once campaigned for racial equality oppose a similar goal—equality for people of each sex. For some citizens sexism is a laughable, frivolous topic. With protests that resemble the fears of racists, some people rail against creating sexual equality and dismantling stereotypes: "All women are going to be forced to get jobs and lose alimony payments." "Freedom from sex roles will destroy the family." "Males and females will be required by law to share the same bathrooms." But the issues of sex roles and sexism have as profound an impact on adolescents' motivation as does racial prejudice.

Many concerns about sexism are beyond the scope of this chapter. But reassurance is available for those who are willing to examine their fears and misconceptions. Awareness begins by understanding that sexism and sex roles are not "women's" issues, any more than racism and racial roles are Indian or Hispanic issues. Both male and female human beings are victims of and participants in sexism. We are pressed into the "masculine" or "feminine" mold, as defined by our culture at a particular point in history. From cradle to grave, most people are treated as "deviants" when they dare to stray too far from their society's dictates about sex roles.

A *sexist* person believes that the behavior and potential of males and females are significantly different and are unalterably determined by genes or hormones. Sexist people may cite philosophical, religious, or "scientific" evidence that the two sexes should not be treated in the same manner and are not capable of the same development. A popular debate is whether the behavioral differences that exist between some males and females are learned or hereditary. For example, are most boys less nurturant with children than most girls because they lack an innate "paternal instinct" or because society discourages nurturance in men? Admittedly the debate cannot be experimentally resolved, since human subjects would have to be totally isolated from any interaction with their species to determine the absolute impact of genetics versus socialization. But research shows that there are more differences among people of the same sex than between the two sexes. Most of the striking differences between male and female behavior are primarily determined by a society's sanctions and roles.[1]

The belief that each sex should be restricted to specific roles is not limited to people from one social class, race, or gender. Sex role stereotypes do vary among the many cultures in America, warranting special attention (See Chapter 7). But people of any color are sexist when they judge males and females by different standards or demand conformity to stereotypic roles. Sexism is not merely inflicted by men against women. There are males and females who punish their own sex as well as the opposite sex for not conforming to sex roles.

In lieu of sex roles that limit the behavior of males and females, another alternative exists–*androgyny*. An androgynous person embodies characteristics of both the old masculine and feminine roles: competitive, athletic, ambitious, independent, assertive, and practical, yet simultaneously cooperative, passive, nurturant, affectionate, intuitive, and dependent. The androgynous spirit defies categorization as masculine or feminine. Nonsexist education and parenting encourages adolescents to develop androgynous personalities by supporting or condemning conduct on the basis of its value for a human being's development and not on the basis of the person's gender. For example, if competitive contact sports contribute to human development, all humans should enjoy those benefits. If nurturing children is a valuable activity, both sexes should participate. Nonsexist adults want to motivate adolescents to develop their talents and to behave without the restrictions of sex roles.

RESEARCHERS' ATTITUDES TOWARD GENDER

Arguments about sex differences and sex roles are complicated by the fact that researchers have historically only studied males.[2] Information on female adolescent development is woefully lacking.[3] Traditionally, this inequity reflects the personal interests of researchers and popularity of questions that were considered relevant only to males: achievement motivation, mathematical skills, aggression, and delinquency. For example, only 5 percent of all federally funded programs on juvenile delinquency in 1975 were related to girls.[4] Some adolescent psychologists continue to ignore recent research about sex differences.[5] Hopefully researchers will devote more attention to female adolescents and to topics generally overlooked for males, such as nurturance and hormonal cycles.

ADOLESCENTS' SEX ROLE ATTITUDES

Much as idealists might like to believe otherwise, statistics suggest that most adolescents' views about sex roles have not changed dramatically during the past twenty years.[6] The majority of female adolescents still opt for social service occupations that shelter them from competition with men instead of the more prestigious, lucrative, and underpopulated "masculine" professions. The tradition prevails that women work in jobs where power is primarily exerted over children or other women. The dream of many young women still reflects visions of their mothers—to marry, have children, and be financially supported by a husband throughout most of adulthood.[7] Other surveys suggest that young adolescent boys are more sexist than girls because they perceive any changes in sex roles as a threat to the status of males.[8] In 1979, 85 percent of one group of high school seniors opposed a wife's employment while the husband cared for their children, and 70 percent disapproved of both parents working if they have preschool children.[9] Some males and females are still unaware that most married women are employed. Although some adolescents are more accepting than previous generations of a man or woman entering nontraditional professions, many are still restricted by their roles and are totally unaware of sexism's impact on their lives. Are males more sexist than females? Rich more sexist than poor? The results of polls are contradictory. The most reasonable conclusion seems to be that no group is categorically immunized against sexism.

At the onset of puberty, sex roles are more rigidly enforced and alter the individual's academic motivation more profoundly than during childhood. Adolescent "tomboys" and "sissies" are seldom tolerated. During adolescence most boys and girls gain increasing respect for masculine characteristics, while devaluing feminine traits and activities.[10]

ADULTS' SEX ROLE ATTITUDES

Although they may espouse commitments to sexual equity, most teachers treat students differently on the basis of their sex. Boys generally receive more praise, more criticism, more punishment, and lower grades than girls for equivalent conduct.[11] Some teachers grade pupils with masculine characteristics more favorably than those with feminine traits.[12] Some male and female faculty members still believe that only men should be principals and that employed mothers cause maladjusted children.[13] Many teachers and counselors are still unaware of their sexist biases or of the revised information about adolescent women's and men's abilities.

LEGISLATION ON SEXUAL EQUALITY

In 1972, almost two hundred years after the Bill of Rights proclaimed that all men were equal under the law, *Title IX* was enacted to request equal education and employment for American females. Unfortunately, many educators and students are still ignorant of their legal rights under this law. Although the government ostensibly disapproves of sexual inequality in education and employment, the spirit of the law is not always embodied.[14] A committee investigating HEW concluded that sex discrimination is generally treated in a cavalier fashion by government officials in order to minimize political controversy.[15] Any citizen has the power, however, to file a Title IX complaint by collecting data and contacting the Department of Education or a state commission of educational equity. Unless people object to educational inequities, Title IX will probably remain more of a specter than a body with muscle or teeth.

THE PRICE OF MASCULINITY

Vocational Development

Some men protest that the price extracted for traditional masculinity is too dear.[16] Most boys are still not free to pursue occupations that may fulfill their personal needs but simultaneously undermine "manliness," such as nursing, teaching preschoolers, interior decorating, hairdressing, or secretarial work. As they age most boys learn that their self-esteem and social status are determined primarily by the prestige of their job or the size of their paycheck. Most adults refuse to honor a boy's request for a baby doll and ridicule men who opt to raise their children while the female parent earns the family's income. A few adventuresome souls are defying the traditional stereotypes of masculinity, but most adolescent boys are still not motivated to explore professions without regard to sex roles or to nurture children.

Personal Development

Some psychologists think that males suffer more anxiety over their sex role and receive more punishment for displaying characteristics of the opposite sex than females. Expressions of emotion (especially tears), nurturance, dependence, acquiescence, passivity, vulnerability, physical affection, fear, or self-doubt are taboo for most boys at any age. Marks of "masculinity" are etched on some young men contrary to their natural grain: athletic prowess, competitiveness, aggressiveness, dominance, ambition, or mathematical or mechanical mastery. Struggling to emulate their heroes, many young men repress or destroy their "feminine" inclinations.

Physical Health

To "act like a man" can literally be lethal.[17] Victimized by demanding careers, financial responsibilities, and repressed emotions, more men than women suffer heart attacks, ulcers, and stress-related diseases. Encouraged to conceal physical and psychological pain, to ignore signs of weakness, and to resolve problems without assistance, many males unintentionally intensify their illnesses. Learning to relate to others without the aid of alcohol and cigarettes, expressing pain candidly and publicly, and rejecting those requirements that create excessive stress may diminish traditional "manliness" but prolong life.

Academics and Discipline

Life in school is less favorable in some respects for boys than for girls.[18] In Germany, where most primary school teachers are men and where reading is considered a masculine activity, boys read better than girls. In America, where reading is usually introduced by females and is often viewed as a feminine skill, boys' reading and learning disabilities outnumber girls' four to one. Living by masculine principles, boys are also more likely than girls to defy school rules, to postpone asking for the teacher's assistance, and to rebel against authority. Consequently they receive more punishment, especially suspensions and physical abuse. Furthermore, if a girl masters a task that boys are stereotypically expected to perform well, she is often applauded for overcoming a "handicap," while boys are seldom commended for their proficiency at feminine tasks.

THE PRICE OF FEMININITY

Vocational Development

Feminine figures are indeed impressive: 85 percent of high school girls will be employed as adults and 33 percent will be divorced. The number of employed mothers has tripled between 1950 and 1976.[19] Despite these realities most girls lower their vocational goals and become less interested in achievement when adolescence begins. Boys are taught that success depends on independence, self-approval, mastery of tasks, competition, and vocational planning. Most adolescent women, however, are urged to establish self-esteem and identity primarily by affiliating with others, achieving intimate relationships, refining social skills, and experiencing pleasure vicariously from boys' achievements.[20] Female training emphasizes compromise, "unselfishness," and cooperation. Although more women entered the labor force during the 1970s than in previous generations, the prestige of their occupations declined.[21] In 1980 the median income for American men was $12,530 and for women $4,920.[22] A primary reason for these financial losses is that most adolescent girls are programmed and educated for part-time jobs and low-paying professions with little opportunity for advancement. Even at the doctoral level most females earn their degrees in the "feminine" disciplines of nursing, teaching, and library science.[23]

Girls who do not abandon their ambitions or who enter nontraditional occupations express fewer sexist attitudes than other young women.[24] These successful girls learn that femininity does not exclude intelligence and ambition. Girls who make the fewest vocational plans are often *vicarious achievers.*[25] They have been taught to derive personal satisfaction from a man's accomplishments rather than to create pride from their own deeds.

Fear of Success

Are girls more afraid to succeed than boys? Studies show that many girls fear success, but that many boys also express anxiety on behalf of males who defy sex role stereotypes.[26] Girls with stereotypic sex role beliefs disapprove of the successful female mainly because they dread the social penalties for her ambition and intelligence. Fear of success ratings did not change significantly during the 1970s despite the growth of feminism. One conclusion from these studies is that many males and females still do not feel free to deviate from cultural restrictions on vocational choice.

Personal Development

Adolescent women become increasingly dependent on approval from others, rather than relying on their own independent judgments and self-evaluations.[27] Most girls learn not to display anger or to assert their views, since these traits in girls are "selfish" and "unladylike." Especially when they are competing against boys, young women usually acquiesce and cooperate rather than display too much ambition, risk taking, or intelligence. While boys' personalities reflect their training to be ambitious, practical, competitive, and outspoken, most girls reflect their training to be sensitive, generous, and loving. The girl's personality usually remains poorly defined, with the expectation that she will adapt to a future husband's and children's needs.[28] Those young women who, like boys, opt to base their identities on their own achievement and independence usually pay the price of extensive social disapproval. Despite their excellent grades, many bright girls become less academically self-confident and less willing to accept personal responsibility for their accomplishments than boys. Many adults have simply not heeded the advice of psychologists who have urged Americans since the 1960s to help adolescent girls become more autonomous and assertive.[29]

SEX ROLES AND MISBEHAVIOR

Why are adolescent boys usually more aggressive than girls? Although some research initially seemed to show that aggression was genetically determined, this assumption has not been clearly demonstrated.[30] Older theorists, including the famous adolescent psychologist Stanley Hall, claimed that adolescent boys were aggressive and delinquent because their sexual drives could not be satisfied. The remnants of this logic linger: "Boys have to sow their wild oats." "He can't control himself, but she can." But the differences in aggression and disobedience between most males and females are more probably a function of the training they have received than of genes or hormones. Most adolescent boys are more likely than girls to be aggressive because they have learned that "masculinity" depends on being physically aggressive, defending a viewpoint, saving face, proving one's strength, accepting dares, challenging authority, defying bullies, demonstrating independence, and establishing dominance.[31]

Unfortunately females are forging ahead into crime and delinquency.[32] From 1970 to 1975 arrests of females increased 56 percent versus 30 percent for males, although only 2 percent of females' crimes were violent. Most young men are punished for adult crimes—larceny, burglary, and theft. Most adolescent women are arrested for defying parents and violating sexual mores. Girls who violate their sex role expectations displease the courts. Consequently the courts overestimate and overprosecute girls for sexual conduct. Once they are incarcerated, girls often receive less vocational and academic training and longer confinements than boys. On the other hand, girls are underprosecuted for aggressive behavior in comparison to boys.

At school boys also pay the piper for their misbehavior more frequently than girls (See Chapter 4). Nevertheless, adolescent women report more guilt, tension, and psychosomatic illness than boys.[33] These reports may simply mean that girls reveal their feelings more candidly than boys. But girls may also be harboring their hostilities and creating tension rather than publicly releasing anger, which would be an "unladylike" act. Boys who are aggressive as children are more apt to continue this pattern as adolescents than girls.[34] Perhaps childhood aggression is sufficiently reprimanded in "young ladies" to have been suppressed by puberty. A boy's delinquency also seems to be more closely aligned to academic failures than a girl's.[35] Apparently a boy's assessment of his self-worth depends more on his academic accomplishments than a girl's does.

One of the most comprehensive studies of delinquent girls identifies several unique aspects of female misbehavior.[36] On the basis of interviews with nearly two hundred delinquents, Konopka concludes that girls become delinquent because of loneliness, academic failure, lack of adult friends, racial prejudice, and sexism. Delinquent girls have not usually received sex education to help them cope with the new responsibilities of sexual conduct, nor have they received vocational training for jobs that satisfy their need for adventure and status. Guided into stereotypically "female" jobs, young women's frustration is increased by the double standard that punishes girls for "behaving like sluts" while ignoring boys for "sowing their wild oats." Society punishes the delinquent girl for violating the cultural definition of femininity as well as for her illegal activities. Unlike delinquent boys, many girls try to escape from their poor self-image and frustration by marrying or by involving themselves in dependent relationships with boys whom they idealize as Prince Charming. Konopka recommends that adults help delinquent girls by providing nonsexist vocational training, eliminating the double standard of sexual conduct, creating some healthy outlets for female aggression, screening adults who work with girls for their sexist prejudices, and improving communication between adults and adolescent women.

NONSEXIST EDUCATION:
Textbooks and Language

When did you last see a woman sleeping in the woods with seven dwarfs guarding her while she waits for a man to wake her with his kiss? Ludicrous? Unfortunately many American textbooks present stories almost as farfetched that supposedly represent reality. In a 1974 survey of 2,760 children's stories, women were portrayed in 14 professions and men in 108.[37] Male leading characters outnumbered females five to one in human stories, two to one in animal stories, six to one in biographies, and four to one in folktales. Similarly, most books have very few examples of unmarried women or single-parent families.[38] Math books usually present female characters grappling with problems in cooking, sewing, and buying food, while males deal with science, money, careers, and sports. Most history books omit females' accomplishments, avoid controversial issues related to sexual prejudice, and generally ignore women's political activities.[39] When textbooks and other curricular materials repeatedly present stereotypes, adolescents' visions for their own motivation and their expectations of other people are narrowed, not expanded.

Another aspect of books that may decrease motivation is sexist language. Some people oppose the elimination of sexist terms, arguing that the issue is trivial or that nonsexist language is "awkward" (Table 8). Words, however, have an awesome power to transmit cultural attitudes: "black" or "nigger," "Spanish" or "spic," "woman" or "chick," "mister" or "boy," "bachelor" or "spinster," "rural" or "redneck." Language conjures up specific images in living color and gender: "men working," "the doctor and his assistant," "the congressmen." Language can influence adolescents' expectations and feelings. Sexist words, like racist words, have sharp edges that can wound individuals and carve restrictive niches for vocational and personal goals.[40]

Librarians, parents, and educators can learn to detect sexual prejudice in adolescent books and curricular materials (Table 9). If new books

TABLE 8. Sexist and Nonsexist Language

Sexist	Nonsexist
chairman	leader, president, head, chairperson
the fair sex, the weaker sex	women, wife, spouse
mailman	mail carrier, postal worker
Mrs. Jones and Bob Smith	Ms. Jones and Mr. Smith
housewife	homemaker
the men and the ladies	men and women, gentlemen and ladies
the breadwinner and *his* family	breadwinners and *their* families
congressman	representative
mankind	human beings, people, humanity
fireman	fire fighter
man-made	synthetic, artificial, manufactured
policeman	police, agent, law enforcer
manpower	human energy, workers, workforce

Note: The terms **he** and **his** should not be used to represent both male and female people.

Source: Adapted from information in **Equal Treament of the Sexes in Books** (New York: McGraw-Hill, 1976).

cannot be purchased, we can still discuss the distortions and stereotypes with students. Librarians are privileged with the unique opportunity to order books and periodicals that offer less restrictive models for adolescents.

Coeducation or Segregation

Some educators believe that adolescent boys and girls benefit from being educated in single-sex schools. Considerable evidence shows that many girls are less assertive, less independent, less talkative, less achievement oriented, and less competitive in coed groups.[41] However, practical obstacles as well as the benefits of coeducation for social development probably deem the idea of segregation a little extreme. Single-sex education should be an available option, however, for students who flourish

TABLE 9. Representative Traits of Nonsexist Books

1. Females are shown in a variety of occupations other than nursing, teaching, and secretarial work.

2. Females face and solve their own problems, and males sometimes seek their assistance.

3. Males show emotions such as tenderness towards children.

4. Females' accomplishments and intellect are emphasized.

5. Derogatory references to those who do not conform to stereotypes (tomboy, sissy, old maid) are omitted.

6. Men and women in nontraditional roles are treated seriously, not as laughable oddities (male nurses, female presidents, male dancers, female truck drivers).

7. Sex discrimination and the feminist movement are discussed as a continuing struggle, not one that ended with the right to vote.

8. It is not suggested that divorce, delinquency, or unemployment are problems created by less restrictive sex roles.

9. Suggestions of genetically determined differences, aside from physical ones, are avoided.

10. Adults who choose never to marry or never to have children are not mocked or pitied.

11. Sexist language is eliminated.

12. There are no suggestions that certain jobs or personality characteristics are appropriate only for one sex.

Source: Based on information in L. Weitzman and D. Rizzo, **Biased Textbooks** (Washington, D.C.: Resource Center on Sex Roles in Education, 1974); "Ten Ways to Analyze Books for Sexism and Racism" (New York: Council on Interracial Books, 1976).

there. Meanwhile, teachers in coeducational classes can modify procedures to discourage sexist patterns and to foster new ways of relating to the opposite sex: assign girls as leaders, periodically arrange segregated groups, design activities that require every person's participation, limit assignments that permit a minority to dominate, discuss dominance and submission with students, praise girls who assume leadership and boys who yield power, and present models of males and females interacting equally. Since adolescent boys have a tendency to dominate and girls often respond passively, our obligation is to help equalize their interactions.

Nonsexist Teaching Strategies

Every educator has the personal power to immediately alter his or her sexist conduct in the classroom and to modify a biased curriculum.[42] Even small gestures like using female examples in math problems improve some students' achievement. If we are dedicated to educational equity, we will have to diligently and candidly monitor our own conduct with adolescents (Table 10). The changes may initially feel awkward but will eventually seem as natural as behaving without racial bias.

A faculty can also model sexual equity for adolescents by reassigning certain faculty responsibilities. We can begin by examining the school's organization: Are the most powerful committees chaired by males? Are social events relegated to female teachers? Are vocational and athletic programs male dominated? Self-study guides are available for schools that are sincerely willing to assess sexual equity.[43] Workshops and con-

TABLE 10. How Sexist a Teacher are You?

---

1. I segregate males and females in many academic and athletic activities.
2. I use textbooks and films that stereotype men and women.
3. I speak and write in sexist terms.
4. I know the rules of Title IX.
5. I assign tasks and lessons on the basis of sex (for example, boys operate media equipment and lift things; girls oversee secretarial and social tasks).
6; I impose different standards of conduct on males and females (boys can fight, smoke, and curse; girls can't).
7. I explain sex roles, sexism, and stereotyping to students.
8. I make fun of "liberated men and women," "women's lib," "effeminate men," "female jocks," and nontraditional roles.
9. I pity girls who aren't pretty, social, or fashionable and boys who aren't athletic, assertive, or mechanically talented.
10. I say things like "Boys shouldn't hit girls," "Ladies first," "Act like a man," and "Ladies don't talk that way" to only one sex and not to the other.
11. I devote more attention to the vocational, mathematical, and athletic development of males than of females.

Note: A nonsexist educator would answer "no" to all statements except 4 and 7.

sciousness-raising activities can also advance nonsexist attitudes. But leaders must conduct discussions on sexism with care. Learn from the mistakes of others who have tried to create educational equity in their schools![44] If efforts to eradicate sexism are mishandled, they can undermine rather than fortify educational equity. Above all, let's share information about sex roles and sexism with adolescents.

Nonsexist Counseling Strategies

Cleverly designed counseling programs are available to help liberate adolescent boys and girls from restrictive roles.[45] Counselors and vocational educators can present statistical facts to dispel unrealistic beliefs about employment, marriage, sex roles, and parenthood. Discussing sex roles has altered the vocational plans and sexist attitudes of adolescents in many projects. Initially, however, adults who counsel adolescents must be willing to confront their own sexist biases and to reeducate themselves (Table 11). A number of counselors are still uninformed about Title IX, biased

TABLE 11. How Sexist a Counselor Are You?

---

1. Do you encourage males and females to explore the same jobs?
2. Do you inquire about boys' future marriage and parenting plans as often as you do girls'?
3. Do you use sexist language or writing?
4. Do the materials in your office depict men and women with non-traditional jobs, personalities, and lifestyles?
5. Have you read about nonsexist counseling methods?
6. Do you use career or personality inventories that are biased?
7. Have you discussed stereotypes with adolescents, their parents, and teachers?
8. Do you consider certain traits "abnormal" for one sex but "acceptable" for the other (sexual activity, physical aggression, ambition, mannerisms)?
9. Do you advocate different punishment for boys and girls?
10. Do you actively encourage students to engage in activities that are traditionally considered appropriate only for the opposite sex?
11. Do you help textbook committees choose nonsexist materials?

Note: A nonsexist counselor would answer "no" to questions 3, 6, 8, and 9.

measurement techniques, the special counseling needs of girls, or theories on sex roles and sex differences. Until we realize that humanistic attitudes will not result in a nonsexist environment, we are unlikely to motivate adolescents to develop the full range of their human abilities.

Questions for Discussion and Review

1. In what respects are racial and sexual prejudice alike?
2. How does sexism influence male and female motivation academically, athletically, and vocationally?
3. In what ways have sex roles remained unchanged from previous decades in America?
4. What surprises you most about Title IX legislation?
5. What are the advantages and disadvantages of the contemporary American male role? The female's role?
6. What frightens you most about encouraging adolescents to develop their personalities without sex role restrictions?
7. How does the vocational, athletic, and academic development of adolescent boys and girls differ?
8. How would you convince an educator or parent to adopt a nonsexist approach for relating to adolescents?
9. How would a nonsexist person respond to the assertion, "There's no harm in males and females behaving the way nature intended"?
10. How can sex roles influence the conduct and treatment of delinquents?
11. What desirable traits of "masculinity" and "femininity" would you encourage in an androgynous human being?
12. How can sexist language and textbooks influence adolescent motivation?
13. How are your own speech, writing, and conduct sexist?
14. What specific changes can teachers, administrators, and counselors make to motivate all adolescents equally?
15. In what situations might coeducation be less motivating than sexual segregation?
16. How might your own life be different if you had received nonsexist counseling, teaching, and parenting during your adolescence?
17. How could you refute the belief that Americans are "absolutely free" to develop their individual personalities and potential regardless of their sex?
18. How might adolescents' lives be enriched if society encouraged androgyny rather than "masculinity" or "femininity"?

A man complained that he couldn't communicate with his teenage son because it was too hard to have a man-to-man talk with a boy wearing one earring.

part three

SPECIAL MOTIVATIONAL PROBLEMS

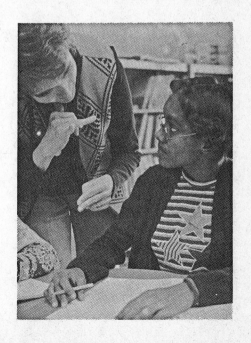

chapter seven

Motivating adolescents from minority cultures

HISTORICAL PERSPECTIVES ON RACISM

In 1954 the Supreme Court ruled that racial segregation in American schools must end "with all deliberate speed." Ten years later President Johnson signed the Civil Rights Bill, outlawing racial discrimination. During these stormy decades, black and white Americans sat-in, spoke out, and stood up to combat racism. However, racist practices and attitudes still subvert attempts to motivate minority youth.

Denying that racism exists is as naive as asserting that no progress whatsoever has occurred toward eliminating discrimination. But in the wake of recent advancements toward racial equity, a disheartening response has emerged: anger from Caucasians who resent the progress of minorities and complain about "reverse discrimination." Complacent over legislation for equality, other Americans have stopped recognizing or combating racism. Prejudice has generally become less blatant and is easier to ignore; yet in many ways our efforts to encourage adolescents from minority groups have barely begun.

RACISM AND ADOLESCENTS

Adolescents are especially vulnerable to racism. Unlike younger children, they are mature enough to recognize discrimination but are too young and powerless to protect themselves or fight back as effectively as adults. Certain forms of prejudice have a particularly profound impact on America's teenaged youth.

Biased Research

Information about adolescents is primarily based on research from white, middle-class boys.[1] Consequently, minority youth often do not receive help tailored to their unique needs and strengths. Prejudice can also influence researchers' interpretations of data. An example is the Moynihan Report, which made sweeping generalizations about black Americans on the basis of data from poor families.[2] Some research on delinquency also exemplifies insensitivity and bias. Many statistics show that middle-class, white boys commit almost as many serious crimes as minorities, but the publicity is toned down because many judges treat richer white boys more leniently than poor ones.[3] Research biases may pass unnoticed by unwary readers and practitioners.

Blaming the Victim

Another way of undermining the motivation of adolescents who are culturally different is to "blame the victim."[4] The group that has power and makes policies can refuse to examine its own conduct and may blame the minority group for not solving its problems: "They ought to pull themselves up by their own bootstraps." Even the victims themselves may eventually be persuaded that their predicaments are solely the consequence of their own weaknesses. Blaming the victim means refusing to accept any responsibility for the economic or educational circumstances of America's poor and uneducated citizens. Members of the dominant group may even believe that the solution to poverty and illiteracy is to rescue minorities from their own "disadvantaged," "deprived" cultures.

The Discriminatory Curriculum

Many textbooks and curricular materials are also discouraging to minorities.[5] Stereotypes of pistol-toting, sombrero-wearing Mexican-Americans and uncivilized, aggressive Indians still flourish. "Indian savages massacred innocent families," but white settlers "cleared the way for progress." Racial bias also means excluding information about minorities' contributions to America and about discrimination that has taken place against nonwhites. Sometimes the only representatives from minority groups are well-behaved individuals who endorse the dominant culture's values, like Pocahontas and George Washington Carver. Those who doubt the impact of a biased curriculum might ask themselves how many nonwhite Americans they can name who have contributed to American culture other than athletes or entertainers.

Athletic Prejudice

Racism also dribbles its way into sports, where equity ostensibly exists among teammates. John Thompson, the coach of a successful college basketball team, explains that white coaches who recruit black players often make racist assumptions.[6] Believing that blacks are undisciplined, many coaches put black players in the "hot dog," one-on-one, freelance positions. Coaches are more likely to train white boys to play in a disciplined fashion. Younger black athletes observe the collegiate teams and fulfill the racial prophecy by following the freelance styles of their older athletic models.

Social Discrimination

People who have never functioned as members of the minority in a group often have trouble recognizing social discrimination. Sometimes individuals who have always been part of the majority say that minorities are "too touchy," "paranoid," or hypersensitive to "imagined" prejudice. Those in the majority may even make the minority youngster who complains about discrimination feel "crazy" or "sick" for imagining nonexistent discrimination. Adults may condescend, trivialize, or joke about a minority adolescent's feelings, totally unaware of how he or she is affected by their "insignificant" remarks and conduct. A daily barrage of small gestures and remarks, which may pass unnoticed by people in the dominant group, nevertheless conveys powerful messages to minorities: "You are not one of us. You are odd. Your group is not as good as ours." Being socially discriminated against sometimes means having others mock your clothes, your physical features, your customs, and your values. It may mean the awkward silence that follows after you enter a room, when everyone abruptly changes the topic or stops laughing. Discrimination may also mean being stared at, talked about, and scrutinized more carefully than members of the dominant group for identical conduct. Put on display as "representatives" of their group, minority adolescents may also feel pressured to perform at a superior level. The first Indian in the debate club, the first black family in the community, and the first girl on the track team may often be living under a bell jar.

Tokenism

Some adolescents from minority groups are treated like tokens. A *token* is any member of a minority who is accepted by the dominant group only on certain terms.[7] Tokens usually try to gain approval by succeeding on the dominant culture's terms. They often have impressive "credentials," either academic, athletic, or intellectual, which cause others to view them as "exceptions to their kind." Often the token is expected to deny membership or close ties to his or her ethnic group or sex. Tokens function as "proof" that the dominant group is not prejudiced, since those in power have apparently included an individual who is not like them. In reality, however, tokens are welcomed only as long as they do not threaten the majority's values. They must not expect that their own cultural or ethnic perspectives will supplant anything in the group that has "accepted" them. Tokenism is a popular and insidious form of prejudice that can demoralize adolescents from minority cultures.

Institutional Racism

Motivation is sometimes diminished by an institution's policies, which may appear perfectly equitable and natural on the surface. Institutional prejudice exists when an organization's practices consistently result in the exclusion or differential treatment of one particular group.[8] Racist or sexist prejudice in institutions such as schools and clubs is usually covert. It consists of policy making that benefits only the group already in power. Goals, standards, measure of success, and punishment are decided unilaterally by the group that has power and by the tokens it has carefully included.

Suppose, for example, that any adolescent in school can join the debating team, which meets at night and wears special uniforms during competition. Unless money is made available to each debater for transportation and uniforms, the club unintentionally excludes talented students from poor families. Another questionable policy is tracking minority and poor youth into classes for the retarded on the basis of intelligence tests, ignoring the evidence that these tests are often an invalid way to estimate intellectual potential. Expelling students from school and corporal punishment are two other policies that create the greatest hardships for poor black boys. The greatest danger is that we will not recognize institutional discrimination, because we tend to focus on more obvious bigotry such as that of the Ku Klux Klan.

Biased Teaching and Counseling

Without intentional malice, counselors often counsel minority youngsters differently from Caucasian youth.[9] For example, assuming that only white boys will become engineers, physicists, astronauts, mathematicians and presidents, many counselors fail to encourage others to achieve their potential. A young Chicana who expresses her interest in biology is counseled to become a nurse, while her white male classmate with similar interests is encouraged to become a surgeon. The issue is not whether Anglo middle-class professions are actually more fulfilling or respectable than other vocations, since that in itself reflects only the perspective of the white culture. The problem is that many counselors advise students on the basis of racial and sex role stereotypes.

By asking minority students fewer questions, lowering academic standards, or keeping greater physical distance, teachers may convey that minorities are less intelligent or less attractive than other adolescents. Adults may even manifest fear of minority youngsters who defy the customs or values of a white, middle-class culture. Grownups communicate disapproval of other races and cultures by approving of minority young-sters who comply with the dominant culture or whose cultural and racial uniqueness is not very apparent.

AMERICA'S RACIAL MINORITIES

A major obstacle to motivating adolescents from racial minorities is that most white Americans know so little about people outside their own economic, religious, or racial group. Although it is foolish and unjust to stereotype every minority person on the basis of his or her ethnic or racial bonds, some fundamental information underscores the special needs and unique values of America's minority cultures.

Black Americans

"Black women have it made!" Sound familiar? Yet, most black girls have to contend with two kinds of prejudice—racism and sexism. In one sense black adolescents are less restricted by their sex roles than other Americans. A woman's self-reliance, economic independence, and edu-cational advancement are traditionally encouraged by black communities, even though approval of female employment and independence arose from economic necessity and not from dedication to feminist principles.[10] Nevertheless, black males and females still need help liberating themselves from sex roles, just as other Americans do.[11]

Most black girls do not generally receive their fair share of educa-tional and vocational encouragement. Nearly two-thirds of black women in professional jobs are in the overcrowded, lower-paid careers of teaching, nursing, and library work.[12] Female scientists from minority cultures say that teachers and counselors seldom encourage minority girls.[13] These scientists encountered both racial and sexual prejudice. They rec-ommend providing role models and internships for adolescent women to work with female scientists.

Despite sexist and racist practices, black females have gradually improved their educational and vocational status.[14] Some observers suggest that educators and employers feel less threatened by black females than by black males, thereby making it somewhat easier for females to advance educationally and vocationally. But black males also are entering jobs that have historically been hostile toward minorities. Black females are also more likely to earn higher grades, graduate from high school, and earn a college degree than black males.[15] However, black girls who graduate from high school earn less money than white or black boys with elementary school educations. The few very educated black women are conspicuous and probably contribute to the myth that being female and black are advantageous, but black girls have problems finding work. In September 1978, adolescent unemployment was 41 percent for black girls, 35 percent for black boys, 15 percent for white girls, and 12 percent for white boys.[16]

Black males also have unique problems related to their race and sex.[17] Young black men are often punished more severely by the judicial system and by schools than white males. These adolescents, discouraged by unemployment and dead-end jobs, often find the armed services their only viable alternative While adolescent white males die most often from car accidents and cardiovascular illnesses, most black males die from murder, suicide, and drugs. Since 1960 blacks between the ages of fifteen and twenty have killed themselves at a higher rate than all other Americans except Indians.

The advances of the 1960s seem to have leveled off for the blacks.[18] While the black middle class has grown, the poorest class has grown faster. Blacks' admissions to law, medical, and professional schools declined between 1973 and 1978. Black adolescents are twice as likely as whites to drop out of high school, three times more likely to be shuttled into classes for the educably mentally retarded, and twice as likely to be one grade behind in school. Black college graduates face about the same chances of unemployment as white high school dropouts.

Hispanic-Americans

America's fastest growing minority group is Hispanic-American. Although about 10 percent of America's population is black, Hispanics will surpass this by the year 2000.[19] Eighty percent of Hispanic-Americans are Mexicans. The remainder are from Cuba and Puerto Rico. Almost all Mexican-Americans live in the Southwest; Puerto Ricans in New York, New Jersey, and Connecticut; and Cubans in Florida. Almost 80 percent of all Hispanics live in cities and work in blue-collar jobs. English is a native language for only 30 percent of these Americans. Their average level of education is 9.3 years, in comparison to 9.6 years for blacks and 12.2 years for whites.[20]

Critics point out that Hispanic adolescents have traditionally been ignored by researchers.[21] Some adults suggest that Hispanic youngsters need special attention for problems unique to their culture. One study, for example, concluded that Hispanics abuse drugs at fifteen times the national average.[22] Hispanic girls also have special problems related to sexism. Only 4 percent of Hispanic girls enter college compared to 8.6 percent of the boys. Like black girls, many Hispanic girls lack role models of successful women and are taught to sacrifice their own needs for their men. Girls from minority cultures are often convinced that their personal advancement will hinder their group by undermining men's progress.[23] Most Mexican-American girls only finish nine years of school compared to the twelve-year national average for other American girls. Most of these young women are less confident, less competitive, less independent, and less educated than Mexican-American boys.[24]

Most Hispanic-American adolescents share a perspective that differs from the Anglo-American view.[25] Motivated by family pride and cooperation, accustomed to respecting their elders, and strictly disciplined, Hispanic youngsters often perceive competition and individual gain as inappropriate. Although the stereotype of "macho" conduct is probably exaggerated, Hispanic sex roles do tend to be more restrictive than those of Anglos or black Americans. Mexican-Americans have often been stereotyped as dependent, unassertive, superstitious, emotional, impractical, and excessively polite. Some critics say that they lack the achievement ethic. Although these traits may represent the differences between Anglo and Mexican-American values, asserting that one culture's perspective is "superior to" another's is a chauvinistic and ethnocentric conclusion.

Of all Hispanic-Americans, adolescents from migrant families are often the most financially and educationally deprived.[26] In 1970, 800,000 children under the age of eighteen were migrant workers on American farms. The migrant worker has a life span twenty years shorter than the average American's. After mining and construction, farm work is the most dangerous labor in America. Many states do not protect adolescents from the educational and physical deprivation of farm labor because agricultural work is exempted from the child labor laws. These adolescents are encouraged to drop out of school to assist their families financially. They frequently must be absent from school to work during the cool mornings in the fields and to move around the country as the crops demand. Most migrant parents are uneducated, poor, non-English speakers who are powerless to change the laws that govern their family's lifestyle. Some school systems are trying to help migrant adolescents by teletyping their health and educational records to each new school. But the National Commission on Migrant Children concludes that most of these youngsters still go to school hungry and suffering from a host of physical maladies.

Native Americans

"No dogs or Indians allowed." Signs of prejudice against American Indians extend farther than racist placards from the Old West. The destruction of sacred burial grounds, broken treaties, massacres, and segregation onto reservations are all part of the Indian adolescent's heritage.[27] (More Indians died in the "Trail of Tears" march to Oklahoma than white people in the Civil War.[28]) In 1972 protesters stormed the Bureau of Indian Affairs demanding that Indians be allowed to participate in the policy-making that governed them. Since 1972 the Indians' desire to preserve their culture has grown. Indians are asking for updated, accurate portrayals of themselves in contemporary America.[29]

Most Indian adolescents live in the Southwestern United States. Two-thirds of Indian children are educated in boarding schools away from their families, due to impassable dirt roads and isolated communities that make local education very difficult. The Indian adolescent is most likely to die from suicide and has the shortest average lifespan of any American. About 60 percent drop out of high school and 25 percent cannot speak English when they begin school at age six.[30] One-third of these youngsters will be jailed during their lifetime and about 35 percent will be placed in foster or state homes. Many have an income of fifteen hundred dollars a year, with unemployment as high as 80 percent on some reservations.[31]

Although white people have tried to "acculturate" minorities, the Native American adolescent's culture retains its uniqueness.[32] Appreciation of nature and respect for the elderly distinguish Indian youth from most other Americans. Competition, ambition, delayed gratification, and orienting each day's activities toward the future are white, not Indian, values. Sharing takes precedence over individual ownership, the family and tribe over the self. Trusting intuition, relying on natural foods and medicines, relaxing, and accepting other people are important; interference with others' cultures, punctuality, and the use of scientific, rational methods are not. Knowledge is not gained solely through formal education, and being a silent listener is as wise as speaking. Respecting manual labor, refraining from criticizing others, cherishing the past, and raising children communally clash with Anglo practices.

Asian-Americans

America's smallest minority represents less than 1 percent of the population.[33] Asian-Americans often intermarry with Anglos and benefit from more flattering stereotypes than other minorities. Chinese, Japanese, and Filipino adolescents complete more years of school than other ethnic groups, and are often channeled into mathematical careers rather than the social sciences. Nevertheless, Asian-Americans have been discriminated against in America. The "Yellow Peril" is a part of the past for many parents of Asian adolescents.

Stereotyped images of the Oriental show an aloof, mathematically minded, formal, obedient human being. Asian adolescents often feel pressured not to "disgrace" their families in any way and may hesitate to ask professionals for assistance. In some Asian communities, adolescents' drug abuse or delinquency is hidden from the outside world in order to preserve families' reputations. Knowing this, professionals need to recognize that many Asian-American youth do have unique problems as members of a minority culture.

WAYS TO ASSIST MINORITY ADOLESCENTS

Although some adults invest time feeling guilty about racial and ethnic prejudice, regret and shame alone do little to motivate minority adolescents. A better investment of energy is to initiate concrete changes to offset some of the inequities and racism in America.

Unbiased Counseling

Many counselors in social service agencies and schools unconsciously counsel from a racist, ethnocentric perspective.[34] The first remedy for this is to become familiar with the minority youngster's culture, rather than treating all clients identically. Counselors should not assume that every black or Hispanic-American will automatically share the same values, since family backgrounds can differ considerably. But by observing the adolescent's conduct, a counselor can notice cultural differences in eye contact, body language, speech, or manner of communicating. Counselors can also ask clients which cultural orientation they prefer, since many adolescents have become *bicultural* in order to function simultaneously in their own group and in Anglo society.

Sensitive, unbiased counselors also recognize that minority adolescents often behave differently from Anglos during a counseling session. Anglo clients are apt to maintain direct eye contact, disclose their feelings without much prodding, initiate conversations, create physical distance during talks, set long-term goals, and arrive promptly for their meetings. When minority youth do not behave in these ways, counselors should not judge them as apathetic or inattentive. Minority youth are more likely to expect specific advice about solving immediate problems and more likely to respect psychoanalytic methods. Long silences are often considered natural in a conversation, rather than "awkward," as Anglos view them. Most Anglo adolescents will be ready to blame problems on themselves, assuming a very internal locus of control attitude. Some minorities, however, do not endorse the idea of an individual "tampering with" fate or nature. Counselors usually want to give students solutions that are based on assertiveness and individual rewards for accomplishments. These techniques will often be unsuccessful with adolescents whose cultures stress passivity or group goals.

The most effective counselors are confrontive as well as empathetic. Confrontation is necessary if minority youngsters are using discrimination as an excuse for not solving any of their own problems. If white counselors continually refuse to hold minority clients accountable for any of their problems, that may be indicating guilt over racial issues. On the other hand, a counselor must not refuse to admit that a prejudiced society does create additional burdens for minority youth. How to straddle two cultures or choose between them are crucial issues for the adolescent to resolve with a counselor's help. Counselors must not assume that their purpose is to help adolescents escape from their "deprived" culture. Half of all minority clients terminate counseling, sensing that their counselors prefer to work with verbal, educated, introspective, self-disclosing people.

Role Models

By introducing adolescents to admirable people of their own race and sex, adults create the possibility for *modeling* to occur.[35] A role model is any individual whom youngsters might admire and identify with enough to imitate. Models can be fictional characters, living people, or historical figures. Caucasian males are surrounded by a vast assortment of models at school, in the community, and in the mass media. Females and minorities, however, usually see only a few stereotypic roles for themselves in textbooks or in the lives of adults around them. Indian physicians, black mathematicians, female scientists, Hispanic authors, or Oriental teachers may never appear in texts or in the community. Consequently, minority adolescents are deprived of models who might expand their vocational and personal options. Unbiased schools provide role models by including people from various ethnic backgrounds on the faculty, in the curriculum, and as guest speakers. Adults can also arrange internships for minority youth with people in the community who volunteer to serve as mentors.

Some schools may claim to be presenting role models already for females and minorities; however, these are often tokens who upheld Anglo values and cooperated with the dominant group in society. Models who truly represent a new cultural perspective, such as Caesar Chavez, are usually excluded from books and schools. To avoid tokenism, adults must choose role models who do not deny the distinct values and practices of their own minority culture.

An Unbiased Curriculum

Although most textbooks and audiovisual materials no longer contain blatantly racist statements, subtle biases persist. An absence of information about minorities and stereotypic portrayals are common. Parents, school personnel, and adolescents can learn to identify biases in the school's textbooks (Table 12). Although financial restraints prevent us from abandoning all prejudiced materials, we can show students the biases and supplement the information. For example, teachers can periodically remind youngsters of prejudices: "Please notice that your science text excludes female and nonwhite scientists. To compensate for this bias, we will be reading from supplementary sources and inviting guest speakers to class." Rating materials on the basis of their sexist and racist perspec-

TABLE 12. Recognizing Racism in Books

1. Does the author assume all readers are white and Christian?
2. Are facts romanticized to glorify the white culture's perspective and to gloss over cruelty and inequity toward minorities?
3. Are minotirites mentioned as social problems rather than as contributors to society?
4. Are minorities described in degrading terms (the "roaming, ferocious, primitive Indians")?
5. Are words used to support a Caucasian perspective without presenting other views (Indians "massacred" but whites "fought battles," white leaders are "assertive and outspoken" but minority leaders are "aggressive and rebellious")?
6. Are the contributions of other cultures ignored? (Is Africa mentioned only in relation to slavery but not in relation to its rich civilizations?)
7. Do evolutionary charts end with a white man, as if he were somehow more truly "evolved" than anyone else?
8. Are oversimplified generalizations perpetuated (fat, eye-rolling Chicana; sombrero-wearing, fiesta-loving bandido; inscrutable slant-eyed Oriental; switchblade-toting Puerto Rican)?
9. Does the minority person progress by adapting to white standards? Is "success" defined only by white male values?
10. Is the oppression of minorities accurately and candidly represented?
11. Does a white person consistently resolve the problems for the minority group member?
12. Are the only nonwhite heroes and heroines people who avoided serious conflict with or contributed to white society?
13. Does the book encourage the passive, patient acceptance of injustice?
14. Do portrayals of nonwhite cultures create genuine respect or perpetuate the "quaint natives in costume" syndrome?
15. If authors and illustrators are not members of the group being written about, is there anything in their background that specifically qualifies them to write this book?

Source: Based upon "How Fair Are Your Children's Textbooks?" (Hyattsville, Md.: National Education Association, 1975); "Ten Ways to Analyze Books for Sexism and Racism" (New York: Council on Interracial Books, 1976).

tives is not designed to censor, but to alert adolescents to the authors' biases.

Creating a multicultural curriculum also can arouse motivation. A *multicultural curriculum* is one that values *cultural pluralism* and does not advocate "melting away" the ethnic and racial differences of Americans.[36] Such a curriculum does not merely tolerate cultural diversity, but actively teaches that ethnic differences are precious resources.

Athletic Equity

Athletic scholarships permit some black males to finance a college education. Athletes can also reap financial rewards from the college diploma that creates professional opportunities. But females from minority cultures seldom profit academically or financially from their athletic talents. As sex roles slowly change, more young women are participating in sports. Creating athletic equity in coaching, finances, equipment, and scholarships might offer minority females more incentives to pursue college educations and more lucrative vocations.[37]

Personal Encouragement

Why do some adolescents succeed despite poverty and prejudice? Some researchers study black youngsters in the ghettos to determine why certain kids remain motivated despite the horrible conditions and crises in their lives.[38] The critical experience that successful children seem to share is a supportive relationship with one adult during their childhood. Adults can create programs that offer every minority adolescent the opportunity to have an adult friend. Clubs, Big Sister and Big Brother projects, and adopted grandparents (retired citizens who volunteer to tutor an adolescent) can boost the morale of minority youth.

Although teachers have too little spare time to develop friendships with many youngsters, an affectionate, reassuring relationship in class is possible. Many minority students have negative or apathetic attitudes towards school. Accustomed to being critized and feeling like outsiders, they are often less able to recognize praise than other classmates. Consequently, adults need to continually encourage disheartened youngsters with written and verbal praise. Unfortunately, as students grow larger, adults' praise usually grows smaller.

Academic Requirements

We render no service to minorities by lowering academic requirements or by lying to parents about their child's skills.[39] Minority youth will remain vulnerable and powerless without the fundamental academic skills that create economic security. Humanitarian efforts to improve self-concepts and to develop ethnic pride are no substitutes for teaching academic skills. Remedial programs in mathematics and reading at the high school level could be used to inspire disheartened adolescents. The most creative, skillful teachers should receive special incentives to teach remedial classes and to work in inner city schools. Counselors also need more training to help teachers remedy minority students' academic problems. When we motivate youngsters academically, we have given them a far greater gift than empathy.

Contingency Contracts

Contracting, or mastery learning, has several special advantages for minority students. By deemphasizing peer competition, contracts are more consistent with some minority cultures' respect for cooperation.[40] Contracts might also protect minority students from discrimination, since the behavioral objectives and consequences are publicly stated at the outset. Properly written contracts preclude a teacher's arbitrary or discriminatory judgments.

Cooperative Environments

Like contracts, peer tutoring and group projects stress cooperation. We can refrain from comparing students to one another publicly and from reinforcing jealous, aggressive spirits. Appealing to family or ethnic pride is often more arousing than forcing minorities to embrace a competitive attitude against others.

Parent Councils

In order to receive federal money, school districts serving Indian communities must have an Indian Parent Council. The committee is not a powerless advisory board, but a policy-making group. The parents implement programs and evaluate personnel who affect their childrens' education. Other minorities could establish similar councils in their communities.[41]

Psychology for Students

Some critics accuse social scientists of helping to maintain the status quo by depriving the least powerful people of the techniques for influencing others. The school's faculty may learn the principles of behavior modification in college courses or in-service workshops, but adolescents remain in the dark. To balance the inequity, we can systematically teach minority adolescents some simple, psychological techniques for influencing adults' conduct.[42] This training may put them in a more powerful position to control their happiness (see Chapter 11).

Institutional Policies

To insure that an organization's policies do not inadvertently demoralize minority adolescents we need to be on the lookout for institutional racism. Intelligence testing, corporal punishment, and suspensions are practices that consistently have the harshest effects on poor and nonwhite adolescents. Achievement tests and instruments to assess specific academic problems are better devices for designing a student's curriculum than a questionable test of intelligence. In-school suspension programs and many disciplinary procedures are more humane, equitable, and effective than suspending or hitting students (see Chapter 4). Careful records of disciplinary actions should show the student's sex and race, the offense, and the consequences for every referral to the principal's office. If minorities are receiving a disproportionate share of referrals or harsh penalties, an advisory committee of students, faculty, and parents should investigate. Regularly reviewing these disciplinary statistics may reveal that certain teachers consistently report more minority students for punishment than others. These teachers need supervision and specific suggestions on modifying their attitudes and classroom procedures. An institution's policies must be periodically examined by outsiders for inadvertent discrimination.[43]

PROFESSIONAL INTEGRITY

Some parents and professionals are afraid to "interfere" with a teacher's classroom practices, a counselor's technique, or an administrator's policies. Such timidity, sometimes referred to as "professional respect," is very unfair to minority youth who are suffering educationally or emotionally in a discriminatory situation. Our loyalties must be to the adolescent's academic progress and mental health, not to colleagues' feelings. Adults, including secretaries and custodians, must be encouraged to discuss publicly any discriminatory conduct against minority youngsters. To remain silent and to protect adults who discourage minority adolescents is to participate in the injustice.

Questions for Discussion and Review

1. What evidence is there that racial and ethnic prejudice still exists in America?
2. What subtle forms of discrimination undermine adolescents' motivation?
3. How many heroes and heroines from American minority groups can you name?
4. What kinds of social discrimination against minorities have you witnessed or heard about?
5. How can individuals know when they are being used as tokens?
6. How can cultural differences influence our attempts to motivate adolescents?
7. How do many teachers and counselors unconsciously discourage adolescents from minority cultures?
8. In what ways have you discouraged adolescents who are from ethnic or racial cultures different from your own?
9. Which adolescents do you believe are most disadvantaged and how would you revise education to meet their needs?
10. If you believe that "reverse discrimination" is a major phenomenon, which minority group and sex would you like to belong to? List all of the advantages which you believe this change would bring you in all the facets of your daily life, such as social status, money, dating, housing, traveling, health, education, and social acceptance.
11. What are some of the cultural differences that may exist between Anglos and Indians? Blacks? Hispanics? Asians?
12. How does multicultural education differ from the idea that America should be a "melting pot" of races and ethnic groups?

13. If a school has decided to examine itself carefully for discriminatory practices, what would you advise the faculty to look at?
14. Aside from the suggestions in this chapter, what could adults do to motivate adolescents from minority groups?
15. Which recommendations in the chapter do you think would be most effective in your community for motivating minority youth?

chapter eight

Motivating adolescents with special needs

GIFTED ADOLESCENTS

Are we prejudiced against intelligent, precocious adolescents? Do we fail to develop the talents of academically gifted students, believing that special classes for them are elitist? Some critics think the answer to both questions is "yes." A primary problem in designing programs for talented youngsters is that contemporary researchers are still undecided about how to define the word *gifted*.[1] Intelligence test scores and teachers' recommendations are often unreliable, especially for identifying gifted girls and minority youth.

The general consensus is that many gifted adolescents are unmotivated and disruptive in school because they are not receiving a curriculum that meets their special needs.[2] Gifted students need freedom to learn at their own rate and to enter college as soon as they are academically ready. The most intelligent youngsters may profit from segregated classes to advance at accelerated rates, but many also benefit from tutoring younger students. Current research does not uphold the old belief that the brightest youngsters need counseling for special psychological or social problems.

Their social skills and personalities are essentially no different from those of their less gifted peers.

Gifted youngsters from minority cultures, however, do have some unique needs and problems.[3] Some adults pay less attention to gifted minority students than to whites with only average skills. Minorities are more likely to be overlooked for placement in advanced classes. Some bright minority youth are perceived as "difficult" children because adults resent their questions or assertiveness. Lacking role models from their own culture, some minority youth feel especially uncomfortable with their intellectual talents. The most intelligent youngsters are also more likely to be aware of prejudice and to be preoccupied with racial or ethnic matters. This awareness may interfere with their functioning in the dominant culture's schools and organizations. Special counseling and a multicultural curriculum help to activate unmotivated minority youth. Counseling may also resolve conflicts arising from a youngster's "double-deviance" as a person distinguished by a minority culture and by above-average intelligence.

Like adolescents from minority groups, young women are less likely to receive encouragement and education for their intellectual talents than Caucasian boys.[4] Precocious adolescent girls must often choose between developing their intellect or behaving as "feminine" people. A bright girl's parents may worry excessively about her social skills and future roles as wife and mother. Both parents and daughters often believe that intelligent girls become socially graceless, unmarried, unattractive women. Even some counselors and teachers are uncomfortable around extremely gifted female students. Adults and adolescents often associate masculinity with the traits of intellectual giftedness: devotion to work, less interest in social events, independence, and assertiveness.

What can educators do to motivate gifted females? Through counseling, personal comments, and the curriculum, we can help girls learn that femininity is not at odds with brilliance. Sex bias and sexist beliefs must be discussed with bright young women. By introducing female role models who are sociable, graceful, and brilliant, we can show girls and boys that intellectual development does not destroy admirable human traits. We must also actively recruit girls into advanced courses, especially math and science, which many have been taught to fear. If possible, we can place adolescent females with mentors for a part of each week. College women and female professionals in nontraditional fields could counsel and encourage younger women. Parents also need our advice on how to encourage their daughters' mental talents (see Chapter 9).

Twelve high schools with twice the national percentage of females in their advanced science and math classes shared two characteristics.[5] The schools actively recruited young women into math and science. The teachers had also been trained to avoid sexist educational practices. With active policies such as these, more bright females will inevitably attain their intellectual potential.

ADOLESCENTS WITH MATH ANXIETY

It just doesn't add up. The costs of math anxiety are dear, yet many grown-ups passively allow students' fears of math to multiply. Adolescents who fear math avoid courses that would greatly expand their future vocational choices and their paychecks.[6] Minority group and female students suffer the worst consequences of math phobia. White males are not necessarily more interested in math, but they are more often forced by parents and educators to continue math courses because "you'll need it in the future to get ahead." The paths to most lucrative careers are paved with mathematical skills.

What causes math phobia?[7] Textbooks typically exclude examples of female or nonwhite mathematicians and scientists. Most students are taught that boys are "mathematically minded," but that girls are talented in literature, arts, and languages. Teachers and counselors often encourage females and nonwhite males to enroll in the less rigorous math courses, assured that these students will not pursue careers in serious science (engineering, medicine, physics). Sports, toys, and games teach boys mathematical skills that girls must then learn at school. Yet schools usually herd the boys into mechanical drawing, shop, science, and math courses, while the girls go into typing, home economics, and languages. Adolescent girls add up the messages and act accordingly: Only 20 percent of the students who continue math beyond high school geometry are girls; only 12 percent of scientific and technical employees are women; and only 7 percent of the doctorates in math are earned by females. Lacking encouragement and role models, many minority males also avoid math and are as handicapped as females.

What is the remedy? To begin with, we can inform students with math phobia that avoiding math classes may cost them financially in the future by limiting their career options. We can also present models of scientists and mathematicians who are not white males, as Newell does in *Black Mathematicians*.[8] Rather than projecting our own anxieties, we can demonstrate enthusiasm about math by supplying math games and puzzles as entertainment. We unconsciously perpetuate math anxiety by assigning mathematical tasks only to boys, by joking about women's inability to balance checkbooks or complete tax forms, and by referring to all mathematicians as "he."

Math teachers have a special opportunity to turn the tables against math phobia. Teachers can discuss anxiety with students by administering a questionnaire to assess tension (Table 13), and can share their techniques for overcoming anxiety. Instead of timing students on how fast

TABLE 13. Math Anxiety Scale

Answer each of the following with a number: 1 = strongly agree; 2 = agree; 3 = not sure; 4 = disagree; 5 = strongly disagree.

1. I enjoy working math problems.
2. I would like to read a biography of a famous mathematician.
3. I would never take math as an elective.
4. I would like to achieve fame as a mathematician.
5. I have no patience for doing math.
6. Math is boring.
7. I often get sleepy in math class.
8. Math helps me solve real-life problems.
9. I like word puzzles better than math puzzles.
10. If a math problem is hard, I keep working at it.
11. I am eager to learn if my math homework is correct.
12. I plan to avoid a career that requires math.
13. I have found interesting books about math in the library.
14. My only reason for taking math is that it is required.
15. I dislike other courses that use math.

Source: Adapted from Sheila Tobias, **Overcoming Math Anxiety** (New York: W. W. Norton and Co., Inc., 1978).

they can work problems, teachers can occasionally disguise math in the form of relaxing games. Students might also analyze their backgrounds to identify when their anxiety began and what factors contribute to their fears. For instance, some adolescents fear a particular type of math problem, timed tests, or a specific concept they never mastered, such as multiplying fractions. An adult might then teach youngsters to overcome those particular problems. Grownups can also help adolescents feel more comfortable about asking questions when they are confused. Manipulative materials such as an abacus or cuisinaire rods also make abstract concepts more concrete and less intimidating. Class discussions should stress the procedures that were used to arrive at both the correct and incorrect answers for math problems.

Some schools create math anxiety clinics.[9] Anxious students meet weekly and complete exercises together. Students sometimes keep a journal, recording their feelings in each day's math class and identifying their specific fears. The group discusses the past to discover the initial causes of math phobias. Assertiveness training shows the timid how to ask questions in math class without shame. Students learn a "Math Bill of Rights": "I have the right to learn at my own pace and not feel put down or stupid if I'm slower than someone else, to ask whatever questions I have, to request extra help, to say I don't understand, to evaluate my math teachers, to be treated with respect, and to define success at math on my own terms." Students who missed as many as one-third of their math classes for one clinic still progressed more than their classmates.

ADOLESCENTS WITH SCHOOL ANXIETY

Sometimes anxiety goes beyond the fear of mathematics. Some adolescents fear school itself, especially tests. Even confident youngsters experience occasional fear or nervousness in some classroom situations. At a minimal level, anxiety helps motivate many youngsters by prodding them to try harder to achieve certain goals. But frequent or excessive anxiety is debilitating and destroys motivation. The more important the task, the more anxious most adolescents become. Some evidence suggests that girls are more worried than boys at school and that the older the child, the more anxiety interferes with performance. Anxious students overestimate how often others are evaluating them and are preoccupied with comparing their performance to everyone else's.[10]

The first step in overcoming school anxiety is to realize that adolescents who appear hostile or apathetic may simply be frightened. Administering a questionnaire helps identify individuals' fears (Table 14). Once these fears are identified, anxious youngsters can usually be helped.[11] Cooperative classrooms which include contracting, programmed instruction, and peer tutoring reduce anxiety. Stating objectives behaviorally, using a criterion-referenced grading system, and deemphasizing speed and time limits also relax youngsters. Teaching self-management skills reduces the likelihood that students will set unrealistically high goals and frustrate themselves (Chapter 11). Most students will perform better after being reassured that failure is a normal part of learning new material or skills. Letting students express their dissatisfaction over unfair test questions also alleviates tension. Well-organized lesson plans with clearly specified behavioral objectives and tasks that do not overemphasize short-term memory are likely to motivate anxious kids.

TABLE 14. Anxiety Questionnaire

---

1. When you have to speak in class, do you worry about what everyone else thinks of you?
2. Do you have bad dreams about school?
3. Do you feel nervous in class during tests?
4. Is it hard to make grades that please your parents?
5. Do you worry about being different from your classmates?
6. Are you afraid to meet new people?
7. Does your hand tremble, your heart race, your breathing speed up, or your body sweat when you have to answer questions or take tests?
8. Do you worry a lot about forgetting what you have learned?
9. After a test, do you continue to worry about how well you did?
10. Are you often afraid that a teacher will punish or embarrass you?
11. Are you afraid to express your opinions in class?
12. Do most of your teachers and classmates seem to like you?
13. While you are taking a test, are you worrying about how well everyone else is doing?

Counselors, parents, and friends can also help adolescents overcome anxiety. Have peer models talk out loud as they take a test to demonstrate the kinds of positive messages that improve performance: "I need to relax and go get some water instead of getting hung up on this one problem." "I know this material and need to quit thinking about how everybody else is doing." Without being hooked up to an elaborate biofeedback machine, adolescents can also learn to control tension by breathing deeply or practicing deep muscle relaxation as soon as their bodies begin to show signs of stress (sweating, shallow breathing, headache, sweaty palms). In deep breathing exercises students are trained to imagine a very relaxing event while concentrating on the slow, rhythmic flow of air into their lungs. Deep muscle relaxation involves training students to tense and relax several major muscle centers until the stressful mental feelings disappear.

In *systematic desensitization,* an adult helps the adolescent write out a hierarchy of fears, beginning with situations that cause no stress and ending with those that create unbearable fear. The counselor explicitly describes the fear-producing situations and the student signals when he or she begins to feel anxious. The counselor then backs up to descriptions that make the youngster feel relaxed and encourages him or her to maintain that relaxation as they try once more to describe anxious situations.

LEARNING-DISABLED ADOLESCENTS

Thousands of unmotivated adolescents who were formerly labeled "slow learners" or "culturally disadvantaged" are now placed in classes for the learning disabled. But what is a learning disability?[12] Technically, students with average intelligence test scores who perform erratically in school are suspected of having a learning disability. While "culturally disadvantaged" adolescents perform poorly in school as a consequence of lack of information and "slow learners" supposedly lack the innate ability to succeed at school, learning-disabled youngsters have the information but cannot process data correctly. The behavior of a learning-disabled student is strikingly similar to that of the slow, disadvantaged, or unmotivated student: short attention span, apathy, discrepancy in ability and performance, misbehavior, academic failure, and inconsistent achievement. Because almost seven times as many boys as girls are labeled "learning disabled," sex role training might contribute to the symptoms. Boys learn to be mischievous, fidgety, inattentive, and defiant, and then must behave passively and obediently in school. Some researchers believe that the label "learning disabled" merely indicates that a student is not performing up to his or her abilities in a particular course.[13] Hence, if we improve our teaching strategies, the learning disability disappears.

When an adolescent is performing poorly in a class, we first want to discover whether any physiological malady is responsible for the problem. Programs for learning-disabled adolescents then advocate *mainstreaming* students into as many classes as possible within the regular curriculum. If a student has dyslexia, which causes the brain to reverse letters or numbers, he or she would probably spend part of each day in a resource room with a special education teacher. But the remainder of the day would be spent in regular classes with the aid of special materials for dyslexic learners.

But how are teachers who have no training in special education supposed to motivate learning-disabled adolescents who are mainstreamed into their classes? Should students be grouped together homogeneously on the basis of their similar academic skills or not? (See Chapter 10.) Fortunately the recommendations for teaching learning-disabled students are similar to the strategies that motivate other classmates.[14] Learning-disabled adolescents need a structured curriculum and classroom activities based on behavioral objectives. The materials should be at the student's reading level and should be supplemented by activities using kinesthetic, auditory, and aural modes. Audio and videotapes and concrete objects to demonstrate abstract concepts (such as an abacus or cuisinaire rods) are useful. Teachers must not rely too exclusively on printed materials to convey information. Learning-disabled students profit from reminders and routines that help them get organized. Lessons should be short, interesting, and accompanied by study guides or test questions to emphasize exactly what is to be learned. Grading should include a variety of projects, not just written exams. Tangible incentives, peer tutoring, criterion-referenced grading, and self-modification techniques are boons for learning-disabled adolescents. These adolescents should not be publicly labeled, separated from their peers, and put in special education classes, for fear of creating self-fulfilling prophecies.

Methods for teaching learning-disabled students are called *precision teaching* or *diagnostic-prescriptive teaching*. The same principles appear in criterion-referenced grading, mastery learning, and contingency contracting. But whichever vernacular we choose, the strategies for helping learning disabled adolescents motivate other classmates as well.

ADOLESCENTS WITH READING PROBLEMS

Why can't many high school graduates comprehend the articles in a *Newsweek* magazine? Because thousands of adolescents are still functionally illiterate.[15] The inability to read appears to be closely linked to delinquency.[16] Yet twenty-four hundred delinquents advanced one full year in reading skills after only four months in "Project Read."[17] These results indicate that poor reading skills are primarily the result of lack of motivation and inadequate education. Having analyzed students' reading performance from 1970 until 1980, the National Commission on Educational Progress recommended that secondary schools invest more time and money teaching adolescents to read. The commission found that even the brightest adolescents read more poorly in 1980 than their peers a decade earlier, partly as a result of teenage employment, large high school classes, and diversions such as television that undermine the motivation to read.[18]

The irony is that although many adolescents read so poorly, simple, inexpensive programs have repeatedly succeeded in motivating young people to read.[19] A boring curriculum whose reading materials are totally unrelated to adolescents' lives does not inspire poor readers to improve. Paperback books on contemporary topics, a library that does not fine students, and attractive advertising for books do motivate poor readers. Providing books on a wide variety of topics and preventing adult interference with adolescents' choices also encourage reading. Schools can sponsor student-operated bookstores where trading paperbacks and buying inexpensive used books are options. Books at school should be promoted occasionally like merchandise in commercial bookstores. Some schools allocate a thirty-minute period each day when everyone in the entire school reads for pleasure. Custodians, secretaries, principals, and teachers read alongside the students. No questions, tests, or discussions follow this exercise. The idea is simply to read for amusement and to develop an affection for books. If a book is boring, the adolescent quits reading and chooses another without any adult reprimands. Censorship is forbidden.

Even adults who do not teach English classes need to arouse more interest in reading. Every high school teacher should learn how to recognize and remedy major reading problems. All teachers can present lists of new words, review their pronunciation and syllabication, and offer special assistance to bilingual students. Peer tutoring, self-reinforcement, and extrinsic rewards will help weak readers to struggle through more difficult reading. Some communities ask retired citizens and unemployed parents to tutor adolescents with reading problems. Tape recordings of books and oral reading by an adult can also accompany silent reading and help adolescents recognize their own errors or learn unfamiliar words without public embarrassment. Adolescents who are given opportunities to help younger children read often improve their own reading skills. Especially with minority youngsters, adults need to be mindful not to create a self-fulfilling prophecy that conveys the message, "You're too stupid or too old to learn to read now."

BILINGUAL ADOLESCENTS

"What's the matter? Can't you understand plain English?" Unfortunately many adolescents cannot.[20] Hispanic adolescents usually learn Spanish as their native language and must compete in school with fewer English skills than their classmates. Native Americans also speak tribal languages on their reservations. Historically all adolescents have been expected to adjust to Anglo-American schools by learning English on their own. Not until 1974 did the Supreme Court rule that schools accepting federal money must provide bilingual classes for students who cannot understand English.

The goal of bilingual education is to improve adolescents' English skills and provide classes in their native language. More bilingual counselors, educators, and social workers are needed to communicate with adolescents and their families whose native language is not English. Research does not substantiate the fear that adolescents who are taught in two languages will become confused. Ideally, the ability to speak two languages should enrich a youngster's life. Too often, however, situations at school and at work are disheartening to an adolescent who is not a native English speaker.

RURAL ADOLESCENTS

Many rural adolescents were ignored until the 1960s when President Lyndon Johnson's "Great Society" programs attempted to bring industry and education into poor rural communities. But many of the antipoverty programs have failed, in part due to the way outsiders and officials condescended to proud rural people and ignored their values and customs.[21] Abandoned factories, mines, and mills have left many rural adolescents' parents with black lung disease, poverty, and sorry schools that drive children away as soon as they can afford to leave. The health care and education of rural adolescents are usually inadequate.[22]

While poverty destroys the motivation of many youngsters, an exemplary educational project called *Foxfire* has motivated students in several rural communities.[23] In 1966 a ninth-grade English teacher, Eliot Wigginton, offered his bored, rowdy classes the chance to produce a magazine and to abandon the traditional English curriculum. These undisciplined, unmotivated youngsters lacked self-esteem as well as many basic English skills. Accepting Wigginton's proposal, the students created a magazine about the local community's history and customs. Interviewing their

relatives and older citizens, they recorded folklore, customs, and personal stories that would otherwise have been lost in oral history. Today's *Foxfire* magazine is thriving, with subscribers in all fifty states and several foreign countries. The students have also created four commercially successful books, record albums containing regional music and live interviews with elderly citizens, television shows, a business to replicate primitive Appalachian furniture, and log playgrounds for elementary schools.

The *Foxfire* project has also inspired youth in other rural communities to preserve their oral history. Navajo adolescents and kids in Maine and Missouri have started their own publications. Mr. Wigginton cautions adults not to let adolescents become so enthusiastic about their own region that they refuse to study other cultures. But his renegade methods have motivated adolescents for over a decade. Believing that the curriculum in most schools ignores real life, Wigginton has given adolescents relevant tasks and responsibilities through which they learn skills in reading, writing, photography, and speaking. Rather than being condescended to or humiliated at school, these youngsters develop self-esteem by interacting with the community, receiving public praise, and developing academic skills as a natural byproduct of their relevant assignments. The students receive full academic credit for their work on the Foxfire projects. Like the tiny organism after which it was named, Foxfire does glow in the dark of the shady mountains.

Questions for Discussion and Review

1. If funds were limited, how would you allocate money for educating gifted adolescents and those with the fewest academic skills?
2. What are your assumptions about the personalities of precocious adolescents? From what experiences are you drawing your conclusions?
3. How would you motivate bright adolescents who are bored with schools?
4. How could we motivate talented female and minority adolescents?
5. What are your feelings about mathematics and how did you develop them?
6. How can adults help students overcome math anxiety?
7. How can we help adolescents combat school anxiety?
8. How can adults lessen an adolescent's test anxiety?
9. What is the distinction between someone with a *learning disability* and a *slow learner?*

10. What methods can teachers use to motivate adolescents with learning disabilities?
11. How could mainstreaming work for or against unmotivated students?
12. How could bilingual education affect adolescents motivation?
13. How have successful programs motivated adolescents to read?
14. What changes could parents and teachers make that would probably improve adolescents' reading skills?
15. How could public schools use adaptations of the *Foxfire* approach to motivate underachievers?

part four

THE INFLUENCE OF FAMILY AND FRIENDS ON MOTIVATION

chapter nine

Assisting adolescents and their families

MYTHS ABOUT FAMILIES

Many adults react to adolescents on the basis of assumptions about their families. For example, teachers may "explain" a boy's selfish behavior by citing the fact that he is an only child in the family. Adults may also give students the benefit of the doubt in ambivalent situations if their parents are wealthy, well-educated members of the community. When communicating with parents, a counselor might automatically assume that black families are matriarchal and consequently talk to the mother as though she were a strong, emasculating female. A nonsexist teacher might also respond with hostility toward Hispanic fathers because she assumes that these men are "macho" figures who dominate women. Because our assumptions about families sometimes influence our conduct toward adolescents or their parents, we can benefit by examining some myths about American families.

The Ideal American Family

Many people judge adolescents and their families by an ideal standard that has not represented reality for decades. This family has two parents, one breadwinner (the father), at least two children, no relatives in the same home, and one person (the mother) who devotes all her time to child-rearing before the children start school. The parents in this ideal family are of the same race, have never been divorced, and have their children before the woman is "too old." If the mother in this family ever seeks employment, it will only be a job that is secondary to her husband's career and her children's needs.

This image of a "good" family still represents the standard against which many people judge themselves and others. But today only one out of every seventeen families has two parents, an unemployed wife, and two children. Almost eleven million children live with only one parent, and almost twenty-eight million children have mothers who are employed. One-fifth of the new babies each year are born to teenaged mothers.[1]

Furthermore, many children grow up in foster homes or institutions without either natural parent. Minority children are especially vulnerable to being separated from their parents and placed in institutions or foster homes. In 1975 twenty-five thousand Indian children attended boarding schools run by the Bureau of Indian Affairs. These schools are miles from the child's home and often reflect disrespect for Indian families. Very little counseling or money is made available to help children and parents remain together. In fact, some researchers conclude that there is a bias against minority cultures which encourages social service agencies to work against preserving or reuniting nonwhite families.[2]

The economic and social realities of contemporary America have created many new varieties of families. Interracial marriage, bachelor fathers, divorced parents, homosexual couples, communal living, unemployed househusbands, unwed couples, and employed women have expanded the narrow definition of the family.[3] Critics who protest that the American family is being destroyed equate the new styles of parenting with chaos and decay. But families that differ from the standards of the white wealthy class are not necessarily unloving or unsupportive environments for adolescents.

Employed Mothers

Many people still believe that a mother who is employed full-time while her children are young is irresponsible and unloving. As a consequence, jobs such as nursing and public school teaching attract many mothers. Another popular expectation is that if a woman works, she must be the parent who takes time off when "her" children need attention. Although these demands are unjust and unrealistic in the contemporary marketplace, many women are made to feel guilty, "unfit," or "selfish" if they dare to violate society's definition of a good mother.

Contrary to the myths, statistics do not show that a mother's employment has negative consequences for her children.[4] Most children benefit when their mothers work for money outside of the home. Adolescents from poor families with employed mothers are no more delinquent than those from rich families with unemployed moms. Children with two employed parents do receive less parental supervision, but they do not react by becoming troublemakers. Housewives' children are often more dependent and more sexist than their peers whose mothers have jobs. Certainly full-time homemakers can be excellent mothers, but so can full-time physicists, professors, bricklayers, plumbers, and truck drivers.

Black Matriarchy

Another popular myth is that black families are matriarchal and that matriarchy is responsible for the plight of black children. *Matriarchy* means that women control the wealth, power, culture, government, and property in a society. According to research like the Moynihan Report of 1965, strong black women preclude the existence of strong black men and children.[5] However, black women do not control the wealth or power in their communities any more than white women do. Most black men have always been and still are the primary decision makers and breadwinners in their families.[6] In 85 percent of low-income families, black women earn less money than black men even though they are usually better educated. Most black women still work in traditionally "feminine" jobs, such as nursing and teaching, that do not threaten the male ego. Furthermore, studies show that a family's income, not race, determines what roles the man and woman will play. Poor families, regardless of race, have similar views on how men and women ought to behave.[7]

Most black children do grow up in homes with two parents, not just with their mother. Income dictates the family's structure more than race; although 70 percent of black families are headed by men,[8] 36 percent with incomes below three thousand dollars are headed by women. Another false and sexist assumption is that a family must be headed by a male in order to be "stable." There is evidence, for example, that women without husbands are more concerned with their childrens' achievements and more supportive than women with husbands.[9] Similarly, two parents are not necessarily more effective than one in preventing delinquency.[10]

Critics point out that the Moynihan Report and other research generally emphasize the weaknesses of minority families and ignore their strengths.[11] Many poor black men were forced to abandon their families because welfare laws withdrew benefits if husbands were present. While black illegitimacy rates are higher than white's, more Caucasians have "shotgun" weddings and falsify medical records to conceal abortions and illegitimate births. Black men and women also seem to be less sexist than whites in supporting women's employment. Many black children raised in poor and racist environments develop an admirable independence and sense of responsibility. Most black families also foster less promiscuous sexual attitudes, create a more supportive network of relatives, and engage in less child abuse than whites.

Undeniably black and white families differ.[12] Black children are three times more likely to have mothers who die in childbirth and two times more likely to die before the age of one than white children. A black child has a 50 percent chance of being born into poverty and of living with only one parent. Black children are more likely to be separated from their parents and put into foster care than whites. But the fundamental difference between white and black families is poverty, not matriarchy.

Poor Families

Income is not the crucial variable that determines whether or not a youngster is being well cared for and loved. Some research even shows that black children raised in ghettos develop such powerful bonds with a loving adult that they are able to withstand situations that would destroy other children.[13] Although outsiders would have judged the adults in these children's lives as "unfit parents," the children profited from and valued the relationship. Nevertheless, some adults blame poor parents for their children's problems, while being less critical of richer parents whose children misbehave or underachieve. Even though poor nonwhite parents are often the most satisfied with schools, many educators tend to view them as adversaries.[14] The vast majority of poor parents favor compulsory attendance and value education despite the mistreatment many of their children receive at school.[15]

Another questionable assumption is that poor parents deprive their children of linguistic and intellectual skills.[16] Critics accuse poor parents of providing so much stimulation at home that their children cannot concentrate or so little stimulation that their kids are dullards. Others accuse parents from lower socioeconomic groups of failing to teach their children how to delay gratification. However, education is usually geared to the needs and learning styles of wealthier students, not to the temperment or values of poor students. Thus, changing our educational practices may motivate more adolescents than clinging to the idea that poor parents have created a linguistically deprived child.

WAYS TO INVOLVE PARENTS IN SCHOOLS

Unfortunately many parents do not feel comfortable around schools. Remembering their own unhappy experiences as students or fearing criticism from professionals, they want to remain uninvolved with social workers and school personnel. What can bridge this gap?

Positive Experiences

One school system regularly advertises meetings for parents and teachers on public radio and in community groceries. Parents can be invited to come to school occasionally just to examine their youngster's textbooks, see the curriculum materials, play with the gym equipment, and visit the cafeteria, bathrooms, locker rooms, smoking areas, and vocational classrooms. Rather than beckoning parents to school only to discuss problems, school personnel should invite parents to celebrate their child's progress.

Communities can also offer services at school that benefit parents personally. Schools can sponsor workshops for parents on how to communicate with adolescents or how to help children adjust to divorce and stepparents. Some school systems also arrange days for parents to visit with teachers from early afternoon until late evening to accommodate the needs of adults who work on evening shifts.

Telephone Services

In another school the teachers tape-recorded a two-minute telephone message each day that gave the homework assignment and summarized the day's class activities.[17] The recording also provided daily attendance figures and general information about special events being sponsored at the school. As a consequence of this project, students' spelling scores and homework improved. The underachievers benefited most. Although a recorded message should not become a substitute for personal conferences, many parents enjoy the privacy, informality, and convenience of such a service.

"Project Excel"

Founded in 1977 by Jesse Jackson as part of "People United to Save Humanity," Project Excel urges parents and youth to sign pledges.[18] Students promise to study two hours each night, to attend school, and to cooperate with teachers. Parents are asked to provide quiet places for their children to study and to prohibit phone calls, television, and music during study hours. Local disc jockeys are asked to cooperate by advertising the importance of an education and by publicly rewarding academic achievers. Reverend Jackson tells youngsters to use the same formula for academics that they use for athletics: daily practice (without the radio), repetition, discipline, sacrifice, and high standards. He insists that because society is racist, minority youth must become "superior" so that they may be considered "average." Jesse Jackson also asks parents and teachers to form committees to advise principals on school policies. Instead of police, parents and coaches should patrol the campus to control violence and vandalism. Parents should also introduce their children to their racial and cultural heritage, encouraging adolescents not to squander the educational opportunities their ancestors fought for. Reverend Jackson's advice motivates many adolescents to improve their academic and social behavior: "A school system without parents at its foundation is just like a bucket with a hole in it. Both tears and sweat are wet and salty, but they render a different result. Tears will get you sympathy, but sweat will get you change."

COMMUNICATION BETWEEN
PARENTS AND ADOLESCENTS

Some parents may need reassurance before their children become teenagers that adolescence is not a declaration of war against adults. Most youth are not swayed by peer pressure except on minor issues like music and fashions. Adolescents' political, religious, and moral values are very similar to their parents' ideas. If parents are verbally reassured by other adults that adolescence is not a dreaded disease, communication with teenagers may become more frequent and comfortable in families.

Advice for Parents

Undoubtedly many parents need a little assistance in learning to communicate with a teenage child.[19] When discussing problems with adolescents, parents should use behavioral statements rather than vague accusations (see Tables 4 and 5). For instance, if an adolescent is not studying, the parent should say, "We have to work out a plan so you will study two hours a night," not "You're lazy and unmotivated." Parents should also avoid comments such as: "You'll never be able to ..." Every cloud has a silver lining." "I don't know why you're so upset." "When I was your age ..." "The trouble with you is ..." Statements like these detract from productive communication by demeaning the adolescent's feelings or condemning his or her whole personality. Naturally parents have the right to express their dissatisfaction and to demand changes. But feelings should be stated candidly and directly without preaching to or exploding at the youngster. The feeling should also be coupled with a specific behavioral complaint: "I feel angry when you only study fifteen minutes a night and you're failing math." "I feel embarrassed when you curse in front of my friends, and I don't want to be around you after you've done that." "I feel happy this week because you got home from school on time and started your homework without my supervising you."

Some parents also need to learn how to listen to their children more carefully before speaking. An effective way to improve a parent's attentiveness is through *reflective listening.* The parent learns to restate the child's feelings and the problem before beginning to speak. For example, an angry son may scream, "You don't love me as much as you love my brother, so just get off my back!" A parent may be too hurt or angry to respond calmly at the moment and can say, "I can tell that you're very upset and so am I. Let's talk about this when we both calm down later in the day." At a later time the parent should restate the child's feelings and try to identify the particular behaviors that are causing the problem: "Earlier today you felt that I did not love you as much as I love your brother. What specifically have I done that makes you feel that way?

Let's talk about what I could do to show you that I love you and what you could do to show that you love me. I feel sad and upset, too."

Wise parents also take care not to mock or minimize their adolescent's feelings. A daughter whose heart is broken over the end of a relationship with her boyfriend does not need to hear, "Cheer up! It's only puppy love!" Although adults do not have to pretend to share the child's perspective, appropriate responses can preserve the adolescent's dignity as well as the parent's right to be candid: "Susan, I know that you must feel the world has ended because you and Herman have broken up. How can we work out some way to make you happier?" Accepting an adolescent's feelings does not necessitate lying or mocking.

Advice for Adolescents

Communication between adolescents and parents is not the sole responsibility of adults. Youngsters can also learn how to understand and relate to their elders.[20] Following the principles of contingency management, adolescents can record their behavior and their parents' responses. By identifying one or two behaviors that frequently annoy their parents, youngsters who change their own conduct can control parents' responses. For instance, after recording all the arguments at home for the past two weeks, a daughter might discover that her father gets angry most often when she forgets to wash the dishes and has to be reminded. The daughter concentrates only on this one behavioral change and records her dishwashing for the next two weeks. She also records her father's responses each evening, especially noting any compliments. In some cases the adolescent may have to be assertive enough to point out the changes for a parent who fails to notice the improvements: "Dad, you don't seem to have noticed that I've done the dishes for six nights without your having to remind me. I'd feel happier if you complimented me for that, because I hate washing dishes but I want you to like me."

Adolescents can also be encouraged to compliment their parents whenever positive changes are occurring. Parents need to feel loved and supported for their efforts to change, and adolescents are in an ideal position to provide this tender, loving care. Brothers and sisters sometimes work cooperatively to compliment a parent for particularly difficult changes: "Thanks, mom, for letting us stay out an extra hour on Saturday nights. That makes us feel like you trust and respect us." "Dad, I appreciate your not yelling at me when I broke the dish. I felt bad about dropping it and I'll be more careful next time." Adolescents who learn to compliment their parents usually have more power and influence over family affairs than those who remain silent.

Family Contracts

Sometimes families need to write their agreements into contracts before problems can be resolved. A family contract is like a contingency contract at school: It must state the behavioral goals and the rewards. Both parents and the adolescent should benefit from a mutually designed contract. Both should receive reinforcement for upholding their end of the bargain. The biggest payoff for both parties is usually that the complaining and arguing end.

COMMUNICATION BETWEEN PARENTS AND PROFESSIONALS

When parents meet with social workers, counselors, or teachers, conflicts or frustration too often result. A conference usually occurs only when the adolescent is in some sort of trouble. Knowing this, all the adults involved are naturally anxious before and during these meetings.

Parents can facilitate conferences about their children in several ways. Before the meeting each parent should write down specific questions he or she would like answered. Rather than becoming defensive if parents ask too many questions or demand that jargon and technical terms be translated into English, competent, empathetic professionals should encourage parents to ask questions and should patiently explain technical terms by providing very specific examples. But parents must be prepared to be persistent with their questions: "I still don't understand why you say my son should be in classes for the learning disabled. Please explain his behavior again for us." "I'm not sure what you mean by contingency contracting. Please show me some examples."

Parents can also help by collecting information at home—for example, how often their daughter studies math and how she responds emotionally to her work. Such specific information can often help adults to devise more effective remedies. Parents should be encouraged to talk with others whose children have similar problems and to read about the topic. If the parents are illiterate, tape recordings can convey information about the nature of their adolescent's difficulties and possible remedies. For instance, if the adolescent is so disruptive in school that all of the teachers' remedies have failed, a contingency contract between the parent, teacher, and student may be the only solution left. Illiterate parents could listen to a cassette tape that explains contracting, accompanied by a simple written sample of a contract. The parents can take the sample home with them, listen to the tape several times on a portable recorder from the school, and return a week later to discuss their questions.

Professionals also have obligations and responsibilities during a conference with parents. By avoiding jargon and providing specific examples in layman's terms, professionals relax parents and create an accurate understanding of the adolescent's behavior. Parents also need specific advice about how to behave with their child at home in order to achieve the specified goals. A wise counselor or teacher brings to the meeting records of such items as tests, homework assignments, number of absences each week, or number of times each day that the child disrupts a particular class. The school should also describe all of the alternatives that have already been tried. A competent professional is obliged to present several alternatives for the parents to consider and to gather specific suggestions from them. The parents and professionals together write out several options and discuss other sources in the community where assistance is available. Adults also need to help each other identify the adolescent's strengths, which can be used to resolve problems. Neither parents nor professionals want conferences to become battlegrounds for attacking and blaming one another. They should try to reassure each other by saying, "We've both probably made mistakes in relating to this youngster, so let's work together from here on."

ADVICE FOR PARENTS WITH DAUGHTERS

Many American parents still prefer to have sons instead of daughters.[21] Yet even those who want a daughter often work against her chances for success and happiness.[22] Reacting to sex role stereotypes, parents may reinforce characteristics in a daughter that undermine her intellectual, vocational, and personal potential. Te richer a girl's parents are and the fewer brothers she has, the more likely it is that she will receive encouragement to develop her mental and physical abilities. Daughters who are the first-born child tend to be more advantaged than other girls because their parents raise them more like sons, encouraging their independence and achievements.

Most daughters are more sensitive to pleasing their parents and more likely to conform to authority than sons. For this reason, parents have an enormous power to influence a girl's attitudes and identity. Specifically, parents need to inform their daughters about the realities of money and marriage, which demand that all adults be financially able to support themselves. By providing nonsexist books and toys and by discouraging girls from reliance on approval from other people, parents foster individuality and self-reliance. If the mother is unemployed, the family needs to make special efforts to invite women into their home who can serve as models of financially successful females. Concerned parents encourage their daughters to solve problems by themselves and to be venturesome. By underemphasizing dating and by supporting athletic and academic activities, adults help their daughters gain vocational and personal skills that will far outlast the benefits of being invited out by boys every Saturday night.

ADVICE FOR MINORITY PARENTS

Most advice on parenting has ignored the special needs of families from minority cultures. Some contemporary researchers, however, offer specific recommendations for parents in interracial marriages or those who are from racial minorities.[23] Some adolescents become so immersed in rhetoric about freedom and racism that they refuse to examine their own shortcomings. A youngster who claims that she is failing three subjects because of racist teachers may need her parent's guidance to recognize that she studies less than fifteen minutes a night. At the same time, loving parents create ethnic and cultural pride by providing nonracist literature and toys at home. If adolescents have begun to stereotype all white people, parents might try acquainting their children with historical and contemporary examples of less prejudiced whites. Parents can help their children recognize racial progress as well as the realities of racism.

Parents may also notice that their children who are attending white schools and living in white neighborhoods have begun to denigrate their own race or culture. Exposing them to more minority role models and discussing tokenism with them are effective tactics. Likewise, black adolescent males may need to be reminded that athletic skills are not as likely to yield financial and social success as academic accomplishments. Daughters must not be taught that their accomplishments undermine the success and self-esteem of males in their ethnic group. The most thoughtful parents empower their children by teaching them how to deal assertively with racism wile developing their intellectual and vocational skills.

Questions for Discussion and Review

1. How can myths and stereotypes about families undermine an adolescent's motivation?
2. What is your definition of a "good" family?
3. What desirable characteristics of your family do not fit the image many people may have of the "ideal American family"?
4. What changes within families are likely to motivate adolescents academically?
5. How can shools improve their relationships with parents?
6. In what specific ways could parents change their behavior to improve communication with adolescents?
7. How could adolescents change their behavior to create more harmony in their families?
8. What kind of family contract could help a son who is not motivated to study at night? A daughter who is not motivated to do her household chores?
9. Role play a parent-teacher conference about a son who is constantly fighting at school. Tape record the conversation. How did each adult impede or facilitate progress? What should have been said or done?
10. How can parents motivate their daughters to become independent, successful adults?
11. In what specific ways do most parents treat their adolescent sons and daughters differently?
12. What family strategies could improve the motivation of minority youngsters?

"If you promise not to believe everything your child tells you happens here at school," wrote the teacher, "I'll promise not to believe everything she says happens at home."

chapter ten

Profiting from the peer group

THE MYTH OF PEER PRESSURE

The adolescent's peers supposedly have the ability to undermine parental guidance, convert angelic youngsters into demons, and render adults virtually powerless with teenagers. Many parents become excessively worried about their child's friendships when adolescence begins. Many books about parenting and adolescent psychology reinforce the image of the impressionable youngster who instinctively yields to peer pressure.[1] The traditional assumption is that the peer group encourages defiance of authority and disregard for adults' values. Authors and teachers who continue to spread exaggerated data about peer pressure are committing an injustice against adolescents.

Research consistently shows that the majority of youngsters do not rebel against their parents or reject their culture's basic values in favor of their friends' beliefs.[2] Most adolescents choose friends from families similar to their own. Peers primarily influence one another's opinions on superficial matters such as music, clothing, hairstyles, curfews, and use of the family's car. The fundamental religious, political, and social principles of most adolescents reflect their parents' convictions. Even young protesters of the 1960s usually manifested their own parents' liberal political convictions. Moreover, peer pressure is not a unique weakness of adolescents. A considerable number of people over twenty are so sensitive to peer approval that they dress, eat, marry, procreate, and vote under the influence of peer pressure. Conformity is the norm in the adult world. "What would the neighbors think!" is an adult fear, not an adolescent one. Undeniably some adolescents are persuaded by their friends to commit illegal, inconsiderate, or self-destructive acts. But, like adults, youngsters differ in their susceptibility to peer pressure.

PHYSICAL SPACE AND PEER INTERACTION

The way adolescents influence their peers is sometimes a consequence of where they sit.[3] When desks are placed in rows with the teacher standing at the front, students in the front row and the center section usually receive more attention than their classmates, which may improve their conduct and grades.[4] Research shows that many adolescents are happier and more involved academically when they are seated next to their peers in a circle.[5] However, the teacher must be sure to maintain eye contact and communication with everyone in the circle. Rows of desks also have the disadvantage of inhibiting a teacher's movement and creating ways for students to hide behind their classmates.[6] To determine which arrangement of desks is most motivating for a particular group, experiment with various seating patterns.[7] Teachers can record the advantages and disadvantages of each pattern and ask for students' opinions. Note carefully how the most timid and the most disruptive individuals respond to each arrangement.

Most adolescents seat themselves according to their friendships, not according to where they can profit most academically. Unfortunately this often separates the least talented learners from the most talented. If the students' choices are undermining academic or social conduct, we should exert our prerogative as a group's leader to reassign new seats. Arrange groups or dyads that are racially, academically, and sexually mixed for specific activities. If someone is socially isolated, seat gregarious people nearby.

MODELING AND ROLE PLAYING

Adolescents are very discriminating when deciding which peers or adults to imitate. Role models are imitated when they are respected by and similar to the adolescent in some significant ways. Youngsters imitate people with whom they can identify and who are receiving attention or rewards that they covet. Superman and Wonder Woman are not role models because they represent supernatural, imaginary characters with very few mortal traits for an adolescent to identify with. For minority or female adolescents, middle-class males like George Washington are also unlikely role models. Adolescent beauty queens, athletes, and cheerleaders may function as role models for their peers who want social status and popularity, while the school's outstanding scholar may be the most influential model for a younger student who values academic achievement.

If we are trying to influence adolescents' conduct, we must choose models they will respect on the basis of their own criteria. Influenced by our own race, gender, and culture, we may unconsciously exclude role models who differ from us but who share much in common with adolescents. The curriculum should include some models for everyone, regardless of cultural, racial, or sexual differences.

Adolescents can resolve many academic and social problems through *role playing*.[8] In role playing, the counselor or teacher describes a situation with which members of the group are encountering difficulty. Then a few adolescents volunteer to improvise a dialogue by assuming one of the roles in the situation. While the audience watches, the youngsters act out the roles and try responding as realistically as possible to resolve the dilemma at hand. After ten or fifteen minutes of role playing, the players and audience discuss the dialogue and decide which responses and resolutions are wisest. Role playing is an attempt to let adolescents profit from their peers' ideas and judgments. The impromptu dialogues encourage everyone to view problems from the perspective of all the parties involved in an experience, not just from one individual's viewpoint.

EDUCATIONAL GAMES

Another way peers can motivate each other is by playing games together. Games not only encourage classmates to model themselves after well-behaved, thoughtful peers, many of them have also improved academic skills or intelligence test scores.[9] Some youngsters have even become less racist after participating in games about prejudice. Advocates of educational games are not suggesting that we abandon the standard curriculum, but that we incorporate games into classroom activities.

Critics warn that too many educators abuse educational games by using games that have no specific academic objectives and no relationship to the rest of the curriculum.[10] Adolescents soon begin to perceive these games as a waste of time. A wise teacher should evaluate each game to decide whether the objectives are relevant to the course and whether the publisher actually accomplishes the goals stated in the advertising. To fulfill academic or counseling goals, adults must discuss a game's significance before and after the group plays it. The same questions that are asked about other academic or counseling activities are relevant after adolescents play games: "What did you learn?" "How does this game relate to what we are studying?" "What errors did you make and how would you correct them next time?" While adolescents play, adults should observe but should not intervene or assist the students. To maximize peer tutoring and modeling, adolescents should play the games with peers of different academic and social skills.

Games on the market today deal with topics as simple as spelling and as sophisticated as racial prejudice. Some games merely require participants to recall factual information from history and literature, while others require players to make judgments about slum landlords and sexual discrimination. Unmotivated adolescents will often master academic skills in order to compete successfully. Shy youngsters may ask questions and seek counsel from their peers during the game. Peers may respect each other's advice and academic information more than an adult's formal instruction. Games create a relaxed, friendly environment in which peers can positively influence and assist each other without the help of adults.

PEER TUTORS AND COUNSELORS

Adolescents are often excellent peer tutors. Research shows that both the tutor and the recipient usually benefit academically.[11] Delinquent students with poor academic records who tutor younger children often improve their own conduct and academic skills. Apparently a sense of self-esteem develops from helping others and from being in a position of authority and responsibility. Some adults purposely choose disruptive adolescents to instruct or lead others as a way of remedying bad behavior. If tutoring is to succeed, everyone must have the chance to teach some skill, and nobody should be allowed to assign grades except the teacher. Even the least talented students can tutor by helping others proofread or recheck their work. The parents of very bright children may also need reassurance that being a tutor is as beneficial as being a student.

Tutoring is effective from elementary through graduate school.[12] Ironically, most tutors benefit more academically than their students. Reviewing academic material, analyzing how learning occurs, and increasing self-esteem by helping others are the most likely reasons for tutors' gains. However, successful programs must allow tutors to develop their own teaching or counseling strategies rather than forcing them to mimic adults. Adults should not treat adolescent tutors like children, but more like colleagues. Tutors need private space for their sessions, access to teachers when they want advice, and time for meetings with other tutors to plan their strategies. Talented young students should not be tutored by slower, older students. Likewise, sex and race can sometimes undermine a tutor's effectiveness. In one program, for example, Mexican-American boys did not respond well to white female tutors. Although ultimate responsibility for modifying and designing the lessons should be left to the tutor, some preliminary training may help tutors avoid major errors.

Tutoring is the basis for a variety of activities. When adolescents are working together on a project, they are actively involved in peer tutoring. Students can also complete their work individually but may ask a classmate to proofread the work before it is submitted to the teacher. Some coaches ask a talented player to teach others who have difficulty with a particular athletic skill, and some counselors arrange friendships in which one student helps another avoid trouble at school. Giving students time to study together for tests and using a criterion-referenced grading system also encourage peers to help each other.

PEER CONTRACTS

Contingency contracts are also effective ways for adolescents to help one another. For instance, two students can negotiate an academic contract: "Susan will teach me to do these equations if I help her study for the history exam. We will tutor each other thirty minutes each day this week." A peer contract can be for social goals: "John will help me quit smoking by keeping track of how many cigarettes I smoke each recess for two weeks. If I reduce my rate by half, John will try to get me a date with his friend Laura." Social contracts can also include an academic skill: "Carla will help me overcome my shyness in math class by telling me what a good job I've done if I speak up. In return I will give her two hours of free tennis instruction every week." We can help adolescents learn to contract with their friends by modeling the process for them: "Mr. Smith, your gym teacher, and I have decided to lose ten pounds each. We're going to run two miles together every afternoon this month. Whoever quits or doesn't show up has to buy the other a lunch." Contracts between adolescents develop interdependence and initiative.

Another form of peer support is a contingency contract based on each group member's conduct. For instance, a teacher can say that when every class member's score on the weekly test improves by five points, everyone will receive thirty minutes of free time on Friday. Critics may protest that using peer pressure in group contracts is unfair because the best-behaved and hardest-working students may be penalized for their classmates' failures. However, a group contract encourages peers to help one another and cooperate to achieve their goals. The method requires everyone to observe his or her own conduct and to assume responsibility for its impact on friends. The class clown might discover that her antics are preventing friends from achieving their personal goals. Haughty, talented students might realize that friendliness and unselfish assistance can help their belligerent, frustrated classmates who interfere with everyone's productivity.

HETEROGENEOUS AND HOMOGENEOUS GROUPING

Is segregating adolescents from their peers on the basis of academic, athletic, or social skills motivating? The vast majority of American secondary schools track adolescents into segregated classes according to academic skills or intelligence test scores. But to track or not to track is a debatable question. [13]

Opponents of *tracking* say segregation creates self-fulfilling prophecies that worsen the conduct and performance of the least talented adolescents and only improve the social and academic behavior of brighter students. Without peer tutoring or models of well-disciplined, hardworking classmates, many lower-track adolescents reinforce each others' bad habits. Despite special equipment, well-trained teachers, and small classes, special education programs have often failed to produce better results than heterogeneous classes. Tracking also separates adolescents on racial and economic terms, since special education and lower-track classes are disproportionately composed of poor and nonwhite students. Another danger of tracking is that some students are misdiagnosed and improperly placed into slow classes.[14] White students with academic problems are far more likely that nonwhites to be placed in classes for the learning disabled rather than classes for the mentally retarded. Some psychologists contend that most adolescents in lower-track classes simply need to be taught how to delay gratification and control their impulsive behavior.

An alternative to tracking adolescents into homogeneous classes is *mainstreaming,* placing students into the least restrictive environment for as much time each day as they can effectively handle. For example, blind youngsters do not need to be segregated from their sighted peers for every class. With some adaptations in the curriculum and physical features of a classroom, they can be mainstreamed into courses with everyone else. A resource room teacher who is trained in special education continues to work individually with mainstreamed students whose needs cannot be met completely in the regular curriculum.

The supporters of tracking argue that pooling students with different abilities into the same classes detracts from motivation. Homogeneous classes allow more individualized instruction and a curriculum suited to special talents or handicaps. There is evidence that some exceptionally smart adolescents flourish in segregated classes where their talents do not cause social problems with peers. Some studies show that youngsters with similar skills are happiest together and that teachers are more pleased with homogeneous groups. Another argument is that if students are mixed together, the brightest dominate the class and make others feel inadequate. In summary, proponents of tracking believe that both the least and the most gifted youngsters profit from segregation.

Where we can take a stand on tracking? A 1979 analysis of American and British researchconcluded that there is no definitive answer to this debate about tracking.[15] These researchers believe, however, that the most exceptionally smart and the least academically talented youngsters are probably the only ones seriously affected by tracking. The underachievers and the least skilled students benefit most from *mixed-ability grouping*. Even the National Education Association stated, as far back as 1968, that there was a lack of evidence to support the practice of ability grouping.[16] If adolescents are too severely handicapped by physical or mental pro blems to profit from heterogeneous classes, then segregation from their peers is a humane alternative. But most adolescents will be more motivated in classes where skills are diverse than in homogeneous classes.

Questions for Discussion and Review

1. How are adults and adolescents motivated by peer pressure?
2. How can seating arrangements affect student's motivation?
3. What determines whose behavior an adolescent is most likely to imitate?
4. How could you justify letting students play games in class to an irate parent who is demanding that schools "get back to basics"?
5. Why does peer tutoring often motivate students?
6. What can cause peer tutoring to fail?
7. How can adolescents help motivate one another using contingency contracts?
8. How can heterogeneous grouping be justified when it seems like a return to the "backward" days of the little red one-room school-house?
9. How can peer pressure be used to motivate youngsters?
10. How can tracking students into special classes work for or against academic motivation?

chapter eleven

Teaching adolescents self-management

FREEDOM AND SELF-MANAGEMENT

Rather than teaching adolescents methods for motivating themselves, we often use psychology only to make youngsters comply with our wishes.[1] Maligned for immaturity and impulsiveness, many youngsters are simultaneously denied opportunities to learn self-management skills. The behavioral psychologist B. F. Skinner recommends that schools teach self-direction, rather than habituating young people to reinforcement from others.[2] Skinner advocates teaching students to set goals and to be free from attention, flattery, and financial offerings from society.

Many of us believe that willpower, self-control, and self-discipline are innate, unalterable characteristics. Consequently, "I have no willpower" becomes a handy excuse for adolescents and adults who fail to achieve their goals. When an adolescent watches television instead of studying or hits another student instead of walking away, "lack of will power" is named as the culprit. "I just couldn't help myself" means "It isn't my fault since I have no will power." In fact, however, the power to control the self is a *learned* skill. We can teach adolescents (and ourselves) specific techniques to increase self-control.[3]

Using self-management procedures means accepting a new definition of the "self."[4] Such statements as "I am aggressive" or "I have a timid personality" imply that self is an entity that cannot be changed; these convictions are contrary to the philosophies of self-management. By learning how to rearrange conditions in the environment and provide rewards for themselves, adolescents have the power to alter many aspects of their personalities, self-concepts, and emotions. By teaching youngsters the techniques of self-management, we discourage them from carelessly abdicating the awesome responsibility of managing their own lives.

OBSTACLES TO SELF-MANAGEMENT

Adolescents with an internal locus of control who know how to congratulate themselves for their achievements learn self-control faster than those who believe external circumstances rule their lives. Before teaching the techniques of self-management we may have to improve an adolescent's locus of control attitude. Some youngsters need to begin self-management with small goals and ample, frequent rewards. Female adolescents who are accustomed to passive reliance and approval from others may need additional practice and encouragement in self-management.

How do we know how much self-management to allow adolescents? Clearly the legal ages for adulthood do not guarantee that someone is capable of making wise, independent decisions. Rather than relying on chronological age, we can ask ourselves several questions about the youngster's behavior and previous experiences. First, has the person already demonstrated the ability to fulfill contracts designed with an adult? If so, he or she is probably ready to learn some self-management procedures. Of course some youngsters who fail to achieve goals that are dictated to them by adults may be very successful at accomplishing their own aspirations with self-management procedures. Second, if the youngster makes a foolish decision, will anyone else be adversely affected? A fourteen-year-old who drives a car may place other humans in jeopardy. Likewise, adolescents cannot be totally free to decide their conduct in a classroom, because those actions have a direct bearing on classmates' learning. The consequences of managing one's own money, academic affairs, diet, or athletics, however, usually only affect the individual who makes the decisions. Third, could any of the adolescent's choices cause irreparable damage to the youngster? An upset stomach from too much beer, a broken arm from a foolish stunt, or a failing grade from insufficient studying are rectifiable and sometimes even instructive. But driving while drunk can be fatal and that, indeed, is irreversible. Fourth, has the adolescent demonstrated the ability to profit from mistakes? If so, he or she is going to benefit from self-management by gradually rectifying errors and refining methods. Fifth, does the youngster have the essential facts to understand the ramifications of each alternative? Some adolescents are well informed. Others lack sufficient information to attempt self-management, such as the unlikelihood of earning good wages without a high school diploma, the divorce rates and financial penalities of early marriage, the statistics on lung cancer and smoking, or the death rates for drunken drivers. For successful self-management, the person must understand the consequences of each choice. Finally, how much experience with independence has the person had at home or in school? Those who have never tried making decisions need more time and practice than those who have had years of directing themselves. Despite these obstacles, delinquents, dropouts, special education students, and the academically gifted have mastered and profited from self-management procedures.

LEARNING TO SET GOALS

Self-control begins by learning to set goals. Because most students are accustomed to following adults' orders, their self-management skills are probably unrefined. We should teach adolescents the principles of contingency contracting before beginning self-management projects.

Setting a goal is a tricky task that is critical to the success of self-control. Most people can quickly identify their aspirations. But people usually fail to achieve goals that are established in a moment of overzealous optimism: "I'll lose forty pounds!" "I'll stop smoking tomorrow." "I'll study twice as many hours every day." We need to help adolescents learn to set realistic goals by discussing specific situations of unreasonable expectations:

Case one: John is a slow reader who made a D in English last term. He has decided to set a goal of turning in two book reports a week for extra credit. Is this a reasonable expectation? (no)

Case Two: Sue wants to lose forty pounds. She usually consumes 3,500 calories a day and does no exercise. Her goal is to eat only one meal daily for the next five weeks and to run a mile each day. Is this a realistic goal? (no)

Case three: Bernie wants to improve his math grade from a C to a B. He now studies math twenty minutes a day with the radio playing. He decides to study without the radio and to add an extra fifteen minutes each day, increasing the time to forty-five minutes after two weeks. Is this reasonable? (yes)

Students should set goals slightly beyond their present performance. Goals should initially span short periods of time, perhaps only one class period. Students must also learn to write their goals in behavioral terms so that measuring progress is easy (see Tables 4 and 5). For example, Susan failed history last year and still hates it. This year she is belligerent toward her new history teacher and refuses to do any work. Her first goal is to make one contribution to a class discussion or to do one written assignment in the next three days. If Sam never participates in gym activities, his first goal might be to play for fifteen minutes without complaining before the week ends. Adolescents may need weeks of practice and supervision to learn how to choose realistic goals and to express them behaviorally.

LEARNING TO OBSERVE THE SELF

"I know what's wrong, but I don't know what to do about it." Most adolescents know exactly what to do in order to remedy a smoker's cough, to play basketball more skillfully, or to lose weight. But other goals are more complicated: "I want my math teacher to like me." "I want to be popular." "I want to overcome my shyness." "I want to stay out of trouble." These vague goals require adolescents to observe their own behavior and the behavior of others so that a specific, narrowly defined goal can be written in behavioral terms. We can help youngsters learn to observe themselves by asking them questions about specific conduct: "What do popular students do that makes others like them?" "What are you doing when your math teacher likes you the most?" "What do other kids do that your math teacher likes?" "What actions get you into trouble?" We might even provide behavioral checklists to help adolescents reach their goals by identifying conduct that they are unaware of (see Table 5).

Once a goal is written the adolescent needs to record each day's progress: "How many calories did I eat at each meal?" "How many laps did I run?" "How many times did I speak in class?" "How many minutes did I study?" "How many times did I compliment the teacher?" Most adolescents record their conduct honestly. Sometimes the mere act of recording changes the youngster's conduct without any further intervention. Initially an adult can record the adolescents' behavior simultaneously and intermittently check the accuracy of the self-recording. Not surprisingly, some young people have not learned to observe themselves objectively. Assist these youngsters by giving them noverbal cues whenever an appropriate act occurs. Raising a finger, writing on a note card taped to the student's desk, or making a mark on the board are cues for the adolescent to self-record. Videotapes and audio tapes are excellent devices for resolving disputes and helping students see their conduct. Requiring adolescents to listen to themselves on a tape and to record their classroom conduct is an excellent way to end a dispute.

SELF-REINFORCEMENT

After learning to set realistic goals and to observe their conduct, adolescents must learn to arrange rewards and penalties for their self-management plan. What incentives will maintain each day's efforts? Rewards can never be too frequent in the initial stages of a self-modification project. A common mistake is to set the goals too high and the rewards too small, too few, and too far in between. Adolescents should arrange daily rewards for themselves as they progress toward their ultimate goal.

Of course penalties also help people resist temptation. Usually just denying oneself the daily reward is punishment enough. For instance, if Susan does not live up to her goal of studying math for thirty minutes, she does not get to telephone her boyfriend. But people who use self-modification have devised other ingenious consequences for failing to meet their daily goals. Some give money to an organization they disapprove of. Others give money to a friend, which is only returned if the daily goals are met. Whatever the method, self-managed people must provide pleasure and punishment for themselves after computing their daily progress.

We can also teach adolescents to write messages to themselves in conspicuous places: "Don't eat, piggy" on the refrigerator door, "Open me to graduate" on a textbook, "Don't raise your voice to this teacher" inside a notebook. Learning to rearrange the physical environment also eliminates some problems. For instance, changing seats in class may help a student reach a goal of finishing classwork on time because he or she no longer sits next to a best friend. We need to help adolescents decide which manipulatable features of the environment are preventing them from achieving their stated goals.

SELF-MANAGEMENT CHECKLIST

If the first self-management projects fail, evaluate the project with the adolescent to be sure that all the essential requirements were there. All the answers to these questions should be "yes" for success:

1. Did you allow yourself ample time to achieve the goal?
2. Do you have the skills necessary to attain such a goal?
3. Did you limit yourself to only one goal?
4. Did you set the goal only slightly above your present level?
5. Did you choose a goal that was in your power to control and that was not dependent upon changes in other people?
6. Did you write your goal in measurable, observable terms?
7. Did you record your behavior daily and accurately?
8. Did you reward yourself daily?
9. Did you reward yourself in large enough doses?
10. Did you rearrange the physical environment to help you reach your goal?
11. Did you increase your goal slowly after beginning to succeed?
12. Did you choose one of the least difficult problems in your life for the first self-management project?
13. Did you provide role models for yourself?
14. Did you have someone help you design your self-management project or practice with you privately before you tried your new skill in public?
15. Did you arrange to have friends reward you?
16. Did you read about others' self-management projects for achieving goals similar to your own?
17. If the goal involved relating to someone else, did you rehearse your new conduct with a friend several times beforehand?
18. Did you try your new skill for the first time around supportive people and at a time when you were most likely to succeed?

19. Did you carry out the negative consequences of not reaching your daily goal?
20. Did you ask some special friends to reward you for your small improvements?

BIBLIOTHERAPY

In conjunction with contingency contracts, adolescents can use books to help motivate themselves. This procedure is called *bibliotherapy*. Literary characters are sometimes persuasive models who offer insights, resolutions, or inspiration.[5] *The Bookfinder* categorizes thousands of books according to themes and reading levels.[6] Films and filmstrips can also help some adolescents solve their own problems. But the force of bibliotherapy depends on accurate, candid portrayals of contemporary problems. If we censor materials or ignore controversial issues, bibliotherapy has little therapeutic value.

STRATEGIES TO CONTROL ANGER

When it is repressed or unleashed, anger can be a demon. Many adolescents' problems at school result from an uncontrollable outburst of anger. Verbal taunting, fistfights, academic apathy, and disrespect to teachers can all be symptoms of anger. One exemplary project for teaching adolescents to redirect or eradicate their anger is "The New Model Me."[7] The curriculum includes workbook exercises, fables, films, and questions on topics such as vandalism, delinquency, violence, peer pressure, and human motivation. Students attempt to become astute observers and evaluators of their own behavior in the midst of frustrating situations: "How did I feel at that moment?" "What did I do?" "What needs of mine were being met or blocked?" "What do I wish I'd done?" "What effect did my action have on others?" The self-observation and questions are very similar to those of reality therapy. Adolescents in "The New Model Me" learn to record each incident in which they successfully control their anger. They also learn to identify and control subtle forms of aggression such as verbal taunting and to empathize with victims of crime or violence. The program can be used by teachers or counselors and is especially suited for junior high school students.

SELF-CONTROL THROUGH SELF-TALK

An adolescent's feelings and consequent behavior are often the results of subjective interpretations of an incident. For instance, one youngster who fails an exam may send herself the message, "I'm too stupid to even try to pass this course so there's no use studying anymore." In exactly the same situation, however, another student may send himself the message, "I've got the ability to do this work, but I really need to go to bed earlier and study harder for the next test." In these situations the messages, or *self-talk,* that the adolescents send themselves are the cause of behavior rather than the event itself. Some thoughtful adults are helping adolescents learn how to control their moods and conduct by changing their self-talk.[8]

Some adolescents have beliefs that encourage them to consistently send negative messages to themselves in almost every situation. By discussing these attitudes, adults can teach adolescents to create more positive messages for themselves in upsetting incidents. A second step is to show kids how to write "counter cards." (see following illustrations).* The cards

---

Irrational: The coach hates me and forces me to train daily as punishment.

Counters:

1. Everyone else in class has to do these exercises too.
2. Training daily is the only way to improve my skill.
3. The coach said my speed was better today than yesterday.
4. Feeling angry will not make me happy or make the coach like me more.

Irrational: There's no use trying to do these math problems.

Counters:

1. Not working cannot possibly improve my grade.
2. I improved my score five points on last week's test after studying.
3. Being depressed cannot help me.
4. I did well in math last year, so I must be exaggerating my problem now.

---

*Source: Based on information from Rian McMullen and Bill Casey, **Talk Sense to Yourself** (Golden, Colo.: Counseling Research Institute, 1975).

list several positive or rational messages which students can take out and read when they find that they are becoming angry or discouraged. The rational sentences counter or block the irrational, debilitating message. As youngsters become more experienced in developing countermessages, they can practice silently repeating the rational sentences to themselves when necessary. Adolescents are even taught to practice saying the positive messages for ten minutes each day and to write down the negative talk that occurs inside themselves whenever they are angry or unhappy. A third technique for altering self-talking is to use a formula for testing thoughts: "My interpretation of this situation is true if ——— and false if ———." For example, an adolescent might decide, "My belief that doing homework is a waste of time is true if most people in this class who did their homework still failed this test, but false if most people who did their homework passed this test." Another youngster might decide, "My feeling that there is no way that this teacher will ever like me is true if nothing changes after I behave politely and smile at him for five days." Teaching adolescents how to create more positive messages means encouraging them to use these procedures daily, until the processes feel natural and automatic.

ASSERTIVENESS TRAINING

Although the meek will supposedly inherit the earth, the timid and submissive adolescent generally loses the riches that come from self-expression. Both timid and belligerent adolescents can reap benefits from assertiveness training.[9] Paradoxically, being assertive sometimes prevents aggression. While aggression is an offensive, belligerent act against others, assertion is a defensive response to protect ourselves from annihilation by an aggressor. Behaving assertively means stating ideas or complaints directly and candidly, but without the condescension, outrage, insults, or public humiliation that usually accompany aggression (Table 15). When being assertive, adolescents should maintain direct eye contact, speak audibly without a hostile or pleading tone, and stand or sit confidently. Teach adolescents to choose a time and place that are quiet and uninterrupted for assertive encounters. The adolescent should discuss only one complaint at a time and should avoid dragging skeletons out of the closet or unearthing ancient history.

There is a test for determining how assertive or passive an adolescent

TABLE 15. Assertive or Aggressive Behavior?

Which of the following represents aggression instead of assertion?

1. "Mr. Jones, I don't understand that problem and I need you to explain it again more slowly before we go on."
2. "This gym class is stupid and boring. I hate this teacher!"
3. "Ms. Smith, I feel bad when you embarrass me in front of the class. What other alternative could we work out?"
4. "I'm not satisfied with my grades and I want to discuss it with you."
5. "I'm angry about the way you graded my paper, but I'd like to talk with you about your evaluation. When do you have time?"
6. "This paper was unfairly graded and I resent your obvious prejudice against me."
7. "Please move me to another table right away. I am allergic to cigarette smoke and you've seated me next to smokers."
8. "I cannot accept your decision. Come over here and look at the mark the ball made when it hit."
9. "I think you are incompetent and I'm not learning anything in your class."
10. "Yes, I do mind if you smoke in here."

Note: Statements 2, 6, and 9 are aggressive.

is. This test asks questions such as: "Are you inclined to be overapologetic?" "Do you ignore them when people push ahead of you in lines?" "If you're studying and classmates are disturbing you, will you ask them to stop?" "If you're angry at someone, can you tell him or her?" "If a teacher makes a statement that you consider untrue, will you question it aloud?" "If a friend makes an unrealistic or unwise request, are you able to refuse?" "Do you freely volunteer your opinions in class?" Adolescents can use this test to pinpoint the specific situations in which their timidity is unproductive.[10]

The philosophy underlying assertiveness training is that adolescents are entitled to express their needs and opinions without feeling guilty or anxious, despite disparities in age, sex, social status, or income. Females and certain minorities may need additional encouragement to behave assertively. Although everyone wisely chooses to behave passively in some situations, the total inability to assert an opinion or a complaint often causes adolescents to become angry or apathetic. Neither feeling enhances motivation. Adolescents who learn to communicate assertively are the most apt to ask for help when they need it and to overcome their debilitating feelings.

SCHOOL SURVIVAL TRAINING

Despite sometimes feeling powerless, adolescents can learn skills to improve their rapport with most teachers. Successful students learn early how to request help politely, smile and nod to indicate approval or understanding, chat with adults, and attend to teachers' personal idiosyncrasies. (Ms. Jones hates chewing gum. The coach detests wet towels on the floor.) Regrettably some students may lack these basic skills, particularly, underachievers or adolescents from cultures whose values differ from the school's. Several programs, therefore, have successfully trained students in "school survival skills."[11]

Youngsters who are accustomed to criticism and academic failure usually underestimate the frequency of adults' approval. By viewing videotapes of interactions between students and teachers, these youngsters learn to recognize compliments from adults. Each week the students in the school survival training group must complete specific assignments in social skills: maintain eye contact with the teacher, sit up straight in class, arrive early to class, ask for the teacher's help, bring materials to class, greet the teacher each day, use the teacher's name, and nod approvingly at the teacher when the student understands a concept. The most important skill for these adolescents to learn is to compliment teachers: "Thanks for explaining that to me again." "I liked this lesson today." Each week the students report the impact these assignments have had on their teachers. Adolescents and the counselor work together to decide which behavioral changes would be most likely to improve teachers' attitudes. The participants in the school survival program eventually learn to recognize the relationship between their own conduct and the teacher's behavior toward them. The adolescents receive many benefits as a consequence of their training program because adults become more willing to spend time with them and genuine rapport has a chance to develop.

We can also teach adolescents how to express themselves in ways that are more likely to persuade adults: First, we must remind them to try to change only one aspect of the school or of an adult rather than attacking the entire system or personality. They should avoid such frightening terms as *destroy* or *get rid of* and instead use terms such as *extend, modify,* or *experiment with*. It is best for them to refrain from obscenities and slogans, but to ask for the rationale underlying unacceptable policies. We can provide suggestions to improve situations when criticizing teachers or rules. A handbook for adolescents, *The Soft Revolution,* shows them how to initiate change within school and become more effective advocates for their own causes.[12]

POWER, PRIDE, AND PROGRESS

Some adults who salute freedom, independence, and democracy may nevertheless feel threatened or uneasy when adolescents try to manage more aspects of their own lives. ("Impertinence is the name which authorities give to the aspirations for and declarations of independence of their inferiors."[13]) We may inadvertently punish assertive, independent adolescents and applaud submissive youngsters for their "maturity." Some of us might dismiss self-control techniques or rebel against adolescents whose independent choices reflect values that differ from our own.

Hopefully we adults will eventually recognize the injustice of berating adolescents for their immaturity, lethargy, or dependence while denying them chances to learn self-management. Hopefully we will endorse self-management even when youngsters' decisions or assertions contradict their elders' choices. Some educators are already ceding more controls to youngsters and encouraging those who are capable of more independence. With instruction in self-management techniques and our applause, more adolescents may unhinge the docile, dependent marionette and cultivate a more autonomous, assertive spirit. Teaching adolescents to control their own motivation is indeed a gift of lifelong value.

Questions for Discussion and Review

1. How do some adults undermine an adolescent's self-management skills?
2. What are behavioral psychologists' views of *willpower* and *the self*?
3. "You can't make a silk purse out of a sow's ear unless you start with

a silk sow." Why do you agree or disagree with this perspective of modifying the self?

4. Which adolescents will be most likely to encounter difficulties with self-management? How could you ameliorate their problems?

5. What are the reasons why so many people fail to fulfill New Year's resolutions and other goals? How can you help adolescents avoid this failure?

6. How can you teach adolescents to observe and assess their own conduct candidly?

7. What kinds of self-management projects can adolescents arrange for themselves in order to improve their grades? to avoid fights? to establish better rapport with teachers?

8. If a self-management contract fails, what might have gone wrong?

9. What is bibliotherapy and why might some communities oppose its use?

10. What specific procedures can you teach adolescents to help them develop control over their anger?

11. How is assertion different from aggression?

12. Describe three situations in which teaching adolescents to behave more assertively could improve academic performance or conduct.

13. How can adolescents use behavioral psychology to improve rapport with adults?

14. When should adolescents be given the freedom to begin learning self-management and over what matters should they have control?

15. How can an adult help adolescents learn self-management by using videotapes, tape recorders, films, or books?

A teenager had a heart-to-heart talk with her father. "Listen, dad, I've come to the decision that it's time for me to stand on my own two feet. But I can't do it on my present allowance."

Notes

Chapter One

[1] John Carroll and Jeanne Chall, eds., *Toward a Literate Society* (New York: McGraw-Hill, 1975), p. 27.

[2] *The Student Pushout* (Atlanta, Ga: Southern Regional Council, 1973); *School Suspensions* (Washington, D.C.: Children's Defense Fund, 1975).

[3] J. Jackson, "In Pursuit of Equity, Ethics and Excellence," *Phi Delta Kappan,* November 1978, p. 92.

[4] Marian Edelman, *Portrait of Inequality: Black and White Children in America* (Washington, D.C.: Children's Defense Fund, 1980), p.9.

[5] Carl Smith and Leo Fay, *Getting People to Read* (New York: Delta Books, 1972), p.8.

[6] *Learning Disabilities: Link to Delinquency* (Washington, D.C.: Health, Education and Welfare, March 1977); E. Gagne, "Educating Delinquents: A Review of Research," *Journal of Special Education, 11* (1977), p. 13-27.

[7] J. Jones, "What Superintendents and School Boards Can Do., *Phi Delta Kappan*, November 1978, pp. 221-23; Thomas Brophy and Jeremy Good, *Looking in Classrooms* (New York: Holt, Rinehart & Winston, 1978), p. 233.

[8] M. Parker, "Case Studies Of the Gifted and Talented Person," in *Educational Guidance of Gifted Students*, eds. P. Perrone and C. Pulvino (Madison, Wisc.: Research Laboratory, 1977), pp. 81-95.

[9]*Changes in Mathematical Achievement 1973-1978* (Denver, Colo: National Assessment of Educational Progress, 1979).

[10]*Three National Assessments of Reading: Changes in Performance 1970-1980* (Denver, Colo.: National Assessment of Educational Progress, 1981).

[11]*Digest of Education Statistics* (Washington D.C.: National Center for Education Statistics, 1980), p. 16.

[12]*Digest of Education Statistics,* p. 14.

[13]*America's Children and Their Families* (Washington, D.C.: Children's Defense Fund, 1979); "Hispanic Youth Employment Needs," *El Noticiero, 20* (1981), p. 4.

[14]*The Educational Disadvantage of Language Minority Persons in the U.S.* (Washington, D.C.: Center for Education Statistics, 1978).

[15]*Digest of Education Statistics,* pp. 6-7.

[16]"The Coleman Report," *The Economist,* April 18, 1981, p. 33.

[17]Christopher Jencks, *Inequality* (New York: Basic Books, 1972).

[18]James Coleman, *Public and Private Schools* (Washington, D.C.: National Center for Educational Statistics, 1981).

[19]Michael Rutter and others, *15,000 Hours* (Cambridge, Mass.: Harvard University Press, 1979).

[20]Bruce Biddle, Jere Brophy, and Thomas Good, *Teachers Make a Difference* (New York: Holt, Rinehart & Winston, 1975).

[21]Evelyn Larton and others, *The Teacher's World* (Washington, D.C.: ERIC Clearinghouse on Teacher Education, 1979); Kevin Ryan and others, *Biting the Apple: Accounts of First Year Teachers* (New York: Longman, 1980).

[22]D. Miller, "What Do High School Students Think of Their Schools?" *Phi Delta Kappan, 57* (1976), pp. 700-702.

[23]W. Fetters, *National Longitudinal Study of the Class of 1972* (Washington, D.C.: Health, Education and Welfare, 1977).

[24]Norman Feather, *Values in Education and Society* (New York: Free Press, 1975).

[25]D. Elkind, "Strategic Interactions in Early Adolescents," in *Handbook of Adolescent Psychology,* ed. Joseph Adelson (New York: John Wiley, 1980), p. 450.

[26]Don Hamachek, *Encounters with the Self* (New York: Holt, Rinehart & Winston, 1978); Bernard Weiner, *Human Motivation* (New York: Holt, Rinehart & Winston, 1980), pp. 415-23.

[27]Marilyn Kash and Gary Borich, *Teacher Behavior and Pupil Self Concept* (Reading, Mass.: Addison-Wesley, 1978), p. 217.

[28]A. Jensen, "The Differences Are Real," *Psychology Today* (Dec., 1973), 80-86.

[29]Ronald Samuda, *Psychological Testing of American Minorities* (New York: Dodd, Mead, 1975).

[30]R. Williams, "The Bitch-100: A Culture Specific Test," *Journal of Afro-American Issues, 3* (1975), pp. 103-16.

[31]M. Pines, "A Head Start in the Nursery," *Psychology Today* (Sept., 1979), 56-64.

[32] Arthur Whimbey, *Intelligence Can Be Taught* (New York: Dutton, 1975).

[33] "Warning Label for Tests," *American Psychological Association Monitor* March 2, 1976, p.8.

[34] "Judge Strikes Down IQ Testing," *American Psychological Association Monitor,* November 1979, p.10.

[35] Weiner, *Human Motivation,* 1980.

Chapter Two

[1] Nancy Seifer, ed., *Nobody Speaks for Me* (New York: Simon & Schuster, 1976); Stephen Joseph, ed., *The Me Nobody Knows* (New York: Avon Books, 1969); Eve Merriam, ed., *The Inner City of Mother Goose* (New York: Simon & Schuster, 1969); Nancy Larrie and Eve Merriam, eds., *Male and Female under Eighteen* (New York: Discar Books, 1973).

[2] James Coleman and others, *Equality of Educational Opportunity* (Washington, D.C.: Health, Education and Welfare, 1966).

[3] Frank Frieri, David Bartal, and Daniel Carrol, eds., *Attribution Theory: Application to Social Problems* (San Francisco, Calif.: Jossey-Bass, 1980); Jerry Phares, *Locus of Control in Personality* (Morristown, N.J.: General Learning Press, 1976).

[4] Phares, *Locus of Control.*

[5] Martin Seligman, *Helplessness* (New York: W. H. Freeman & Company Publishers, 1975).

[6] T. Chandler, "Locus of Control: A Proposal for Change," *Psychology In The Schools,* 1975, *12,* 334-39; B. Weiner, "A Theory of Motivation for Some Classroom Experiences," *Journal of Educational Psychology,* 1979, *71,* 3-25; C. Ames, R. Ames, and D. Felker, "Effects of Competitive Reward Structure on Achievement Attributions," *Journal of Educational Psychology,* 1977, *67,* 1-8; C. Diener and C. Dweck, "An Analysis of Learned Helplessness," *Journal of Personality and Social Psychology,* 1978, *36,* 451-62; G. Fanelli, "Locus of Control," in *Motivation In Education,* ed. Samuel Ball (New York: Academic Press, 1977), pp. 45-63.

[7] William Glasser, *Reality Therapy* (New York: Harper & Row, Pub., 1965).

[8] Alvyn Freed, *Transactional Analysis for Teens and Other Warm Important People* (Sacramento, Calif.: Jalmar Press, 1976); Stan Woolams and Michael Brown, *The Total Handbook of Transactional Analysis* (Englewood Cliffs, N.J.: Prentice-Hall, 1979).

[9] Ken Ernst, *Games Students Play* (Milbrae, Calif.: Celestial Arts, 1972).

[10] Louis Raths, Merrill Harmin, and Sidney Simon, *Values and Teaching* (Columbus, Ohio: Chas. E. Merrill, 1965).

[11] Richard Reichert, *Self Awareness Through Group Dynamics* (Dayton, Ohio: Pflaum-Standard, Inc., 1970); William Pfeiffer and John Jones, *Structured Experiences for Human Relations Training* (Iowa City, Iowa: University Press, 1971).

[12] Richard DeCharms, *Enhancing Motivation* (New York: Irvington Press, 1976).

[13] K. Deaux, "What Is Skill for the Male Is Luck for the Female," *Journal of Personality and Social Psychology*, 1974, *29*, pp. 80-85.

[14] S. Erkut, *Sex and Race Effects in the Attribution of Achievement*, American Psychological Association, August, 1978; H. Farmer, "Career Counseling for Lower Social Classes and Women," *Personnel and Guidance Journal*, April 1978, pp. 467-71; C. Rosen, "Impact of an Open Campus on High School Students' Sense of Control," *Psychology in the Schools*, 1977, *2*, 216-18.

[15] *Women's Athletics* (Washington, D.C.: Clearinghouse on Teacher Education, 1976), p. 23.

Chapter Three

[1] Commission on the Reform of Secondary Education, *The Reform of Secondary Education* (New York: McGraw-Hill, 1973). Reprinted by permission of the publisher.

[2] William Bechtol, *Individualizing Instruction and Keeping Your Sanity* (Chicago: Follett, Inc., 1973); Robert Glaser, ed., *Adaptive Education: Individual Diversity and Learning* (New York: Holt, Rinehart & Winston, 1977).

[3] Bernard Weiner, *Human Motivation* (New York: Holt, Rinehart & Winston, 1980), p. 391.

[4] Thomas Good and Jeremy Brophy, *Looking In Classrooms* (New York: Holt, Rinehart & Winston, 1978), pp. 250-78.

[5] Nathan Ausubel, *Educational Psychology: A Cognitive View* (New York: Holt, Rinehart & Winston, 1968); Joel Levin, *Learner Differences: Diagnosis and Prescription* (New York: Holt, Rinehart & Winston, 1977); Janet Moursund, *Learning and the Learner* (Monterey, Calif.: Brooks/Cole, 1976), pp. 262-93.

[6] Walter Dick and Lou Carey, *The Systematic Design of Instruction* (Glenview, Ill.: Scott, Foresman, Inc., 1978); James Block and Lorin Anderson, *Mastery Learning in Classroom Instruction* (New York: Macmillan, 1975).

[7] Garth Blackham and Adolph Silberman, *Modification of Child and Adolescent Behavior* (Belmont, Calif.: Wadsworth, 1975); Gene Ramp and George Semb, eds., *Behavior Analysis: Areas of Research and Application* (Englewood Cliffs, N.J.: Prentice-Hall, 1975); Robert Williams and Kamala Anandam, *Cooperative Classroom Management* (Indianapolis: Bobbs-Merrill, 1974); Vernon Jones, *Adolescents with Behavior Problems* (Boston: Allyn & Bacon, 1980); James Long and Virginia Frye, *Making It Till Friday* (Princeton, N.J.: Princeton Press, 1977).

[8] Norman Gronlund, *Stating Objectives for Classroom Instruction* (New York: Macmillan, 1978); Lloyd Homme, *How to Use Contingency Contracting in the Classroom* (Champaign, Ill.: Research Press, 1976).

[9] B. Ware, "What Rewards Do Students Want?" *Phi Delta Kappan*, January 1978, p. 355.

[10] Frank Taylor, Alfred Artuso, and Frank Hewett, *Motivating Reluctant Learners* (Denver, Colo.: Love Publishers, 1974).

[11] C. Schultz and R. Sherman, "Social Class, Development and Differences in Reinforcer Effectiveness," *Review of Educational Research, 46* (1976), pp. 25-59.

[12] Bernard Staw, *Intrinsic and Extrinsic Motivation* (Morristown, N.J.: General Learning Press, 1976).

[13] Michael Rutter and others, *15,000 Hours* (Cambridge, Mass.: Harvard University Press, 1979).

[14] Marilyn Kash and Gary Borich, *Teacher Behavior and Pupil Self Concept* (Reading, Mass.: Addison-Wesley, 1980).

[15] R. Farason, "Praise as a Motivational Tool," in *Human Dynamics in Psychology and Education*, ed. Don Hamacheck (Boston: Allyn & Bacon, 1977), pp. 64-68.

[16] David Johnson and Roger Johnson, *Learning Together and Alone* (Englewood Cliffs, N.J.: Prentice-Hall, 1975); William Glasser, *Schools without Failure* (New York: Harper & Row, Pub., 1969); Howard Kirschenbaum, Sidney Simon, and Rodney Napier, *Wad-ja-get: The Grading Game in American Education* (New York: Hart Publishing Co., 1971), pp. 251-92.

[17] David Chamberlain and others, *Adventures in American Education* (New York: Harper & Row, Pub., 1942).

[18] Good and Brophy, *Looking*, p. 251.

[19] Rutter, *15,000*, p. 198.

[20] J. Jellison and J. Harvey, "Why We Like Hard, Positive Choices," *Psychology Today*, March 1976, pp. 46-49.

[21] Good and Brophy, *Looking*, p. 27.

[22] William Hill, *Learning Through Discussion* (Beverly Hills, Calif: Sage Publications, Inc., 1969); William Kryspin and John Feldhusen, *Analyzing Verbal Classroom Interaction* (Minneapolis, Minn.: Burgess, 1974).

[23] C. Jencks, "The Wrong Answer for Schools Is Back to Basics," *Washington Post*, February 19, 1978, p.6.

[24] "A Challenging, Changing Twelfth Grade," *National Association of School Principals Bulletin*, September 1979, pp. 1-12.

[25] Dale Baughman, *Baughman's Handbook of Humor in Education* (West Nyack, N.Y.: Parker Publishing Co., 1974); Antony Chapman and Hugh Foot, eds., *It's a Funny Thing Humor* (Elmsford, N.Y.: Pergamon Press, 1977).

[26] Paul Insel and Lenore Jacobsen, eds., *What Do You Expect: An Introduction to Self-Fulfilling Prophecies* (Menlo Park, Calif.: Cummings Publishers, 1975).

[27] Robert Rosenthall and Lenore Jacobsen, *Pygmalion in the Classroom* (New York: Holt, Rinehart & Winston, 1968).

[28] Jeremy Brophy and Thomas Good, *Teacher-Student Relationships* (New York: Holt, Rinehart, Inc., 1974).

Chapter Four

[1] B. Bayh, "Seeking Solutions to School Violence and Vandalism," *Phi Delta Kappan*, January 1978, pp. 229-302.

[2] S. Neill, "Violence and Vandalism," *Phi Delta Kappan*, January 1978, pp. 302-7.

[3] W. Grant and C. Lind, *Digest of Educational Statistics: 1976* (Washington, D.C.: Health, Education and Welfare, National Center for Educational Statistics, 1977).

[4] Neill, "Violence," p. 305.

[5] Bayh, "Solutions," p. 301; John DeCecco and Arlene Richards, *Growing Pains: Uses of School Conflict* (New York: Aberdeen Press, 1974).

[6] National Institute of Education, *Violent Schools, Safe Schools: Report to the Congress* (Washington, D.C.: U.S. Government Printing Office, 1978).

[7] M. Gold and R. Petronio, "Delinquent Behavior in Adolescence," in *Handbook of Adolescent Psychology*, ed. Joseph Adelson (New York: John Wiley, 1980), pp. 495-536.

[8] Gold, "Delinquent Behavior."

[9] *Children Out of School in America* (Washington, D.C.: Children's Defense Fund, 1974).

[10] *School Suspensions: Are They Helping Children?* (Washington, D.C.: Children's Defense Fund, 1974); *The Student Pushout* (Atlanta, Ga.: Southern Regional Council, 1973).

[11] *America's Children and Their Families* (Washington, D.C.: Children's Defense Fund, 1979), p. 8.

[12] D. Duke, "How Administrators View the Crisis in School Discipline," *Phi Delta Kappan*, January 1978, pp. 299-302.

[13] "Alternatives to Suspension," *Practitioner*, April 1977, pp. 42-49.

[14] *Suspensions and Expulsions: Current Trends in School Policies and Programs* (Arlington, Va.: National School Public Relations Board, 1976); *Discipline in Our Big City Schools* (Washington, D.C.: National School Board Association, 1977); *The Best of Creative Discipline* (Columbia, S.C.: American Friends Committee, 1980); James Oliver, *Forty Positive Preventative Prescriptions for Those Who Care* (Burlingame, Calif.: California Association of School Principals, 1977).

[15] David Johnson, "Conflict Management in the School and Classroom," in *Social Psychology of Education*, eds. Daniel Bar-Tal and Leonard Saxe (New York: Halstead Press, 1978), pp. 214-30.

[16] L. Nielsen, "Successful In-School Suspension Programs," *The School Counselor*, May 1979, pp. 325-31; Bruner Mizell, *Designing a Positive In-School Suspension Program* (Columbia, S.C.: American Friends Committee, 1977).

[17] G. Sewall, "Chasing Ghosts," *Newsweek*, August 24, 1979, p.44.

[18] *Discipline in Big City Schools.*

[19] David Elkind, "Strategic Interaction in Early Adolescence," in *Handbook*, ed. Adelson, pp. 432-71.

[20] C. Jacobson, "Secondary Schools and Student Responsibility," *Phi Delta Kappan*, January 1978, pp. 338-41.

[21] D. Brooks, "Contingency Contracts with Truants," *Personnel and Guidance Journal*, January 1974, pp. 316-20.

[22] S. Macdonald and R. Gallimore, "Contingency Counseling by School Personnel," *Journal of Applied Behavior Analysis, 3* (January 1970), pp. 175-82.

[23] "Mass Truancy Hearings," *Your Schools*, December 1975, pp. 16-17.

[24] *National Congress of Parents and Teachers Report* (Washington, D.C.: National Association of School Principals, 1976).

[25] *National Center for the Study of Corporal Punishment Journal* (Philadelphia, Pa.: Temple University, 1977); *Task Force Report on Corporal Punishment* (Washington, D.C.: National Education Association, 1972); *A Manual on Nonviolence and Children* (Philadelphia, Pa.: American Friends Peace Committee, 1977); Frank Brown and others, *The Reform of Secondary Education* (New York: McGraw-Hill, 1973), p. 20.

[26] M. Levine, "Are Teachers Becoming More Humane?" *Phi Delta Kappan*, January 1978, p. 353.

[27] Julia Vargas, *Behavioral Psychology for Teachers* (New York: Harper & Row, Pub., 1977), pp. 163-83; Michael Rutter and others, *15,000 Hours* (Cambridge, Mass.: Harvard University Press, 1979), p. 185.

[28] Brown, *Reform*, p. 20.

[29] Marcia Macbeath, *Little Changes Mean a Lot* (Englewood Cliffs, N.J.: Prentice Hall, 1980); Charles Madsen and Clifford Madsen, *Teaching Discipline* (Boston: Allyn & Bacon, 1981); Vernon Jones, *Adolescents with Behavior Problems* (Boston: Allyn & Bacon, 1980); Vargas, *Psychology for Teachers*.

[30] F. Medway, "Causal Attributions for School Related Problems," *Journal of Educational Psychology*, 1979, *71*, 809-18.

Chapter Five

[1] Boston Women's Health Collective, *Our Bodies, Ourselves* (New York: Simon & Schuster, 1978); Sam Julty, *Men's Bodies, Men's Selves* (New York: Dial Press, 1979); Ruth Bell, *Changing Bodies, Changing Lives: A Book for Teens on Sex and Relationships* (New York: Random House, 1980).

[2] M. White, "Effects of Nutrition on Educational Development," in *Motivation in Education*, ed. Samuel Ball (New York: Academic Press, 1977), pp. 173-88; J. Frost and B. Payne, "Hunger in America," in *The Disadvantaged Child*, eds. Joe Frost and Glenn Hawkes (New York: Houghton-Mifflin, Inc., 1970), pp. 70-83.

[3] Saul Miller and Joane Miller, *Food for Thought* (Englewood Cliffs, N.J.: Prentice-Hall, 1979).

[4] J. Brody, "So Now It's Perilous to Breathe Indoors," *International Herald Tribune*, February 5, 1981, p. 1.

[5] M. Diamond, "Uppers and Downers in the Air," *Psychology Today*, January 1980, p. 128.

[6] M. Fogel, "Auto Fumes May Lower Your Kid's IQ," *Psychology Today*, January 1980, p. 108.

[7] J. Jorgensen, "An Alternative to Suspension for Smoking," *Phi Delta Kappan*, *57* (1976), p. 549.

[8] Don Hamacheck, *Encounters with the Self* (New York: Holt, Rinehart & Winston, 1978), pp. 112-45; Marilyn Kash and Gary Borich, *Teacher Behavior and Pupil Self Concept* (Reading, Mass.: Addison-Wesley, 1978), pp. 63-99.

[9] Daniel Offer, Eric Ostrov, and Kenneth Howard, *The Adolescent: A Psychological Self Portrait* (New York: Basic Books, 1981); A. Peterson and B. Taylor,

"The Biological Perspective of Adolescence," in *Handbook of Adolescent Psychology*, ed. Joseph Adelson (New York: John Wiley, 1980), pp. 117-55.

[10] Shirley Cohen, *Special People* (Englewood Cliffs, N.J.: Prentice-Hall, 1977); John Gliedman and William Roth, *The Unexpected Minority: Handicapped Children in America* (New York: Harcourt Brace Jovanovich, Inc., 1980).

[11] James Shaver and Charles Curtis, *Handicapism and Equal Opportunity* (Reston, Va.: Council for Exceptional Children, 1981).

[12] Donald Sabo and Ross Runfola, eds., *Jocks: Sports and Male Identity* (Englewood Cliffs, N.J.: Prentice-Hall, 1980).

[13] *Importance of Equal Athletic Opportunity* (Washington, D.C.: Project on Status of Women, March 1978).

[14] Bonnie Parkhouse and Jackie Lapin, *Women Who Win: Exercising Your Rights in Sports* (Englewood Cliffs, N.J.: Prentice-Hall, 1980).

[15] Sheila Tobias, *Overcoming Math Anxiety* (New York: W.W. Norton & Co., Inc., 1978).

[16] Stephanie Twin, *Out of the Bleachers: Writings on Women and Sports* (New York: McGraw-Hill, 1979).

[17] F. Harper, "Outcomes of Jogging: Implications for Counseling." *Personnel and Guidance Journal*, October 1978, pp. 72-78; R. Driscoll, "Exertion Therapy," *Behavior Today*, 6 (1975), pp. 10-16.

[18] E. Snyder, "High School Athletes and Their Coaches," *Sociology of Education*, 45 (1972), 313-25.

[19] "Some Heavy Facts about Teenage Sexuality" (Washington, D.C.: Center for Population Options, 1980).

[20] *Options* (Washington, D.C.: Center for Population Options, Fall 1980), page 2.

[21] *Options*, p. 2.

[22] Reuben Pannor, Fred Massarik, and Byron Evans, *The Unmarried Father* (New York: Springer Publishing Co., 1971).

Chapter Six

[1] Eleanor Macoby and Carol Jacklin, *The Psychology of Sex Differences* (Stanford, Calif.: Stanford University Press, 1974); Hillary Lips and Nina Colwill, *The Psychology of Sex Differences* (Englewood Cliffs, N.J.: Prentice-Hall, 1978).

[2] Joseph Adelson and Margery Doehrman, "The Psychodynamic Approach to Adolescents," in *Handbook of Adolescent Psychology*, ed. Joseph Adelson (New York: John Wiley, 1980), p. 114; President's Science Advisory Committee, *Youth: Transition to Adulthood* (Chicago: University of Chicago Press, 1974), p.7; Daniel Offer and Judith Offer, *From Teenage to Youg Manhood* (New York: Basic Books, 1975).

[3] Max Sugar, ed., *Female Adolescent Development* (New York: Brunner/Mazel, 1979), p. ix.

[4] Task Force on Women, *Little Sisters and the Law* (Washington, D.C.: Law Enforcement Assistance Administration, 1975), p. 10.

[5] Eric Erickson, *Identity: Youth and Crisis* (New York: W.W. Norton & Co., Inc., 1968).

[6] *Women in Search of Equality* (Princeton, N.J.: Educational Testing Service, 1979), p. 10.

[7] *Expanding Adolescent Sex Roles* (Ithaca, N.Y.: Department of Science Education, Cornell University, 1978), p. 45.

[8] Marcia Guttentag and Helen Bray, *Undoing Sex Stereotypes* (New York: McGraw-Hill, 1976)

[9] "You've Come a Long Way Baby, Until a Baby Comes Along," *Coping with Women*, Spring 1979, University of Michigan, p. 5; G. Ditkoff, "Stereotypes of Adolescents Towards Working Women," *Adolescence, 54* (1979), 277-82.

[10] B. Hanes, R. Prawat, and S. Gussim, "Sex Role Perceptions During Adolescence," *Journal of Educational Psychology*, 1979, *71*, 850-55.

[11] Expanding Roles, *p. 36.*

[12] M. Bernard, "Does Sex Role Behavior Influence the Way Teachers Evaluate Students?" *Journal of Educational Psychology, 71* (1979), pp. 553-62.

[13] Myra Sadker, ed., *Jill Came Tumbling After: Sexism in American Education* (New York: Harper & Row, Pub., 1973).

[14] *Stalled at the Start: Government Action on Title IX* (Washington, D.C.: National Organization of Women's Legal Defense Fund, 1978).

[15] *Enforcing Title Nine* (Alexandria, Va.: U.S. Commission on Civil Rights, 1980).

[16] Joseph Pleck, ed., *Men and Masculinity* (Englewood Cliffs, N.J.: Prentice-Hall, 1974); Joseph Dubert, *A Man's Place: Masculinity in Transition* (Englewood Cliffs, N.J.: Prentice-Hall, 1980); James Doyle and Richard Moore, *Attitudes Toward the Male's Role* (Washington, D.C.: Catalogue of Selected Documents in Psychology, 1978), p. 35; Albert Tolson, *The Limits of Masculinity* (New York: Harper and Row, 1977); Mark Fasteau, *The Male Machine* (New York: McGraw-Hill, 1976).

[17] Herb Goldberg, *The New Male: From Self Destruction to Self Care* (New York: David Morrow, 1979); Meyer Friedman and Ray Rosenman, *Type A Behavior and Your Heart* (New York: Fawcett Crest, 1974).

[18] *Expanding Roles*, p. 36; J. Glidewell, "Psychological Context of Distress in School," in *Social Psychology of Education*, Daniel Bartal and Leonard Saxe, eds., (New York: Halsted Press, 1978), p. 167; R. Gordon, "Ties That Bind," *Project Peer Newsletter*, July 1980, p. 4.

[19] *Women Workers Today* (Washington, D.C.: Department of Labor, 1976).

[20] B. Brackney, "The Psychology of Female Adolescents," in *The American Woman*, Marie Abbott, ed. (Holt, Rinehart & Winston, 1979), pp. 133-60; Irene Frieze, *Women and Sex Roles* (New York: W. W. Norton, 1978), p. 248; Daniel Offer, Eric Ostrov, and Kenneth Howard, *The Adolescent: A Psychological Self Portrait* (New York: Basic Books, 1981).

[21] *Social Indicators of Equality for Minorities and Women* (Washington, D.C.: U.S. Commission on Civil Rights, 1979).

[22] *Money Income and Poverty Status of Families and Persons in the U.S.: 1980* (Washington, D.C.: Department of Commerce Census Bureau, 1980), p.2.

[23] *Doctoral Degree Awards to Women* (Washington, D.C.: National Center for Education, 1979).

[24] H. Farmer, "What Inhibits Achievement and Motivation in Women," in *Counseling Women*, Lenore Harmon, ed. (Monterey, Calif.: Brooks-Cole, 1978), p. 166.

[25] J. Lipman and H. Leavitt, "Vicarious and Direct Achievement in Adulthood," *Journal of Counseling Psychology*, 1976, *6*, pp. 26-32.

[26] M. Horner, "Toward an Understanding of Achievement Related Conflicts in Women," *Journal of Social Issues*, 1972, *28*, pp. 157-75; D. Tresemer, "Fear of Success: Popular but Unproven," *Psychology Today*, March 1974, pp. 82-88.

[27] N. Feather, "Values in Adolescence," in *Handbook*, ed. Adelson, pp. 273-84; *Female Adolescent Development*, 1979; *The Adolescent*, 1981.

[28] J. Marcia, "Identity in Adolescence," in *Handbook*, ed. Adelson, p. 179; Juanita Williams, *Psychology of Women* (New York: W. W. Norton, 1979).

[29] Lynn Kovar, *Faces of the Adolescent Girl* (Englewood Cliffs, N.J.: Prentice-Hall, 1968).

[30] M. Abbott, "Early Socialization of the Female Child," in *The American Woman*, ed. Marie Abbott (New York: Holt, Rinehart & Winston, 1979), pp. 102-5; John Money and Amelia Ehrhardt, *Man Woman, Boy Girl* (Baltimore, Md.: Johns Hopkins University Press, 1972).

[31] Macoby and Jacklin, *Sex Differences;* Lips and Colwill, *Sex Differences.*

[32] Freda Adler, *Sisters in Crime: The Rise of the New Female Criminal* (New York: McGraw-Hill, 1975).

[33] A Locksley and E. Douvan, "Stress on Male and Female High School Students," in *Adolescent Behavior and Society,* ed. Rolf Muuss (New York: Random House, 1980), pp. 175-91.

[34] J. Kagan and H. Moss, *Birth to Maturity* (New York: John Wiley, 1962).

[35] B. Haney and M. Gold, "The Juvenile Delinquent Nobody Knows," *Psychology Today*, September 1973, pp. 49-55.

[36] Gisella Konopka, *The Adolescent Girl in Conflict* (Englewood Cliffs, N.J.: Prentice-Hall, 1966).

[37] *Dick and Jane as Victims* (Princeton, N.J.: Women on Words and Images, 1974).

[38] Catherine Horner, *The Single Parent Family in Children's Books* (Metuchen, N.J.: Scarecrow, 1978).

[39] *Stereotypes and Distortions in History Books* (New York: Council of Interracial Books, 1973); Howard Zinn, *People's History of the United States* (New York: Harper & Row, 1980).

[40] Robin Lakoff, *Language and Woman's Place* (New York: Harper & Row, Pub., 1975).

[41] Richard Schmuck and Patricia Schmuck, *Group Processes in the Classroom* (Dubuque, Iowa: Little-Brown, Inc., 1979), p. 71.

[42] D. Sadker, *Being a Man: Activities on Male Sex Role Stereotyping* (Washington, D.C.: Office of Education, 1978): *Expanding Adolescent Sex Roles*, 1978; Barbara Gates, *Changing Learning Changing Lives* (Old Westbury, N.Y.: Feminist Press, 1978); C. Ahlum and J. Fralley, *High School Feminist Studies* (Old Westbury, N.Y.: Feminist Press, 1976); *Changing Sexist Practices in the Classroom* (Washington D.C.: American Federation of Teachers, 1978); *Nonsexist Education for Survival* (Washington, D.C.: National Education Association, 1973); *Today's Changing*

Roles: Nonsexist Teaching (Washington, D.C.: National Foundation for Improvement of Education, 1974).

[43] S. McCune and M. Mathews, *Rate Yourself and Your Institution* (Washington, D.C.: Resource Center on Sex Roles in Education, 1975).

[44] M. Verheyden, *A Handbook for Workshops on Sexual Equity in Education* (Washington, D.C.: American Personnel and Guidance Association, 1976); Barbara Harrison, *Unlearning The Lie* (New York: Liveright, 1973).

[45] Cecelia Foxley, *Nonsexist Counseling* (Dubuque, Iowa: Kendall-Hunt, 1979); Barbara Gutek, ed., *Enhancing Women's Career Development* (San Francisco, Calif.: Josey Bass, 1979); Sunny Hansen and Rita Rapoza, eds., *Career Development and Counseling Women* (Springfield, Ill.: Charles Thomas, 1978); Lenore Harmon and others, eds., *Counseling Women* (Monterey, Calif.: Brooks-Cole, 1978); Dorothy Jongeward and Drew Scott, *Women as Winners* (Reading, Mass.: Addison-Wesley, 1979); Karen Schaffer, *Sex Role Issues in Mental Health* (Reading, Mass.: Addison-Wesley, 1980).

Chapter Seven

[1] Joseph Adelson, ed., *Handbook of Adolescent Psychology* (New York: John Wiley, 1980), p. xi; Robert Guthrie, *Even the Rat Was White: A Historical View of Psychology* (New York: Harper and Row, 1976).

[2] Robert Staples, *Introduction to Black Sociology* (New York: McGraw Hill, 1975); Michele Wallace, *Black Macho and the Myth of Superwoman* (New York: Dial Press, 1978).

[3] M. Gold and R. Petronio, "Delinquent Behavior in Adolescence," in *Handbook*, ed. Adelson, pp. 495-536.

[4] William Ryan, *Blaming the Victim* (New York: Random House, 1972).

[5] *Stereotypes and Distortions in History Books* (New York: Council on Inter-racial Books, 1973); Howard Zinn, *The People's History of the United States* (New York: Harper & Row, 1981).

[6] B. Gilbert, "The Gospel According to John," *Sports Illustrated* (December, 1980), 89-102.

[7] J. Laws, "The Psychology of Tokenism," *Journal of Sex Roles, 1* (1975), pp. 51-67.

[8] Joe and Clarice Feagin, *Discrimination American Style* (Englewood Cliffs, N.J.: Prentice-Hall, 1978).

[9] Derald Wing Sue, ed., *Counseling the Culturally Different* (New York: John Wiley, 1981).

[10] Joyce Ladner, *Tomorrow's Tomorrow: The Black Woman in White America* (New York: Doubleday, 1972); D. Ford, "Counseling for the Strengths of Black Women," in *Counseling Women,* ed. Lenore Harmon (Monterey, Calif.: Brooks-Cole, 1978), pp. 118-40; A. Harrision, "Black Women," in *Toward Understanding Women,* ed. Virginia O'Leary (Monterey, Calif.: Brooks-Cole, 1977). pp. 136-45.

[11] "A New Black Struggle" *Newsweek,* August 27, 1979, pp. 58-69.

[12] *The Educational and Occupational Needs of Black Women* (Washington, D.C.: National Institute of Education, 1975).

[13] S. Malcolm, P. Hall, and J. Brown, *The Double Bind: Price of Being a Minority Woman in Science* (Washington, D.C.: American Association for the Advancement of Science, 1976).

[14] J. Gump and L. Rivers, "A Consideration of Race in Efforts to End Sex Bias," in *Issues in Sex Bias and Sex Fairness in Career Interest Measurement,* ed. Edward Diamond (Washington, D.C.: Health, Education and Welfare, 1975), p. 139.

[15] Project on the Status of Women, *Minority Women and Higher Education* (Washington, D.C.: Association of American Colleges, 1976).

[16] A. Herman, "Still Small Change for Black Women," *Ms.,* February 1971, 96-98.

[17] R. Staples, "To Be Young, Black and Oppressed," *The Black Scholar,* December 1975, pp. 2-9.

[18] Marian Edelman, *Portrait of Inequality: Black and White Children in America* (Washington, D.C.: Children's Defense Fund, 1980); *Money Income and Poverty Status: 1980* (Washington, D.C.: U.S. Commerce Department Census Bureau, 1981), p.2.

[19] "Mexico," *The Economist,* April 18, 1981, p. 45.

[20] R. Ruiz, "Cultural and Historical Perspectives in Counseling Hispanics," in *Counseling the Culturally Different,* ed. Derald Wing Sue (New York: John Wiley, 1981), pp. 186-216.

[21] Amado Padilla and others, *Hispanic Mental Health Bibliography* (Los Angeles, Calif.: University of California Mental Health Research Center, 1978).

[22] Amado Padilla and others, *Inhalant, Marijuana and Alcohol Abuse Among Barrio Children and Adolescents* (Los Angeles, Calif.: University of California Mental Health Research Center, 1977).

[23] P. Vela, "The Dark Side of Hispanic Women's Education," *Agenda: Journal of Hispanic Issues,* May 1978, p. 10.

[24] *The Educational and Occupational Needs of Hispanic Women* (Washington, D.C.: National Institute of Education, 1976).

[25] Joe Martinez, ed., *Chicano Psychology* (New York: Academic Press, 1977); Alfredo Castenada, Richard James, and Webster Robbins, *The Educational Needs of Minority Groups* (Lincoln, Nebr.: Professional Educators, Inc., 1974).

[26] Ronald Taylor, *Sweatshops in the Sun* (Boston: Beacon Press, 1973).

[27] Vine Deloria, *God Is Red* (New York: Grosset & Dunlap, 1973).

[28] E. Richardson, "Cultural and Historical Perspectives in Counseling American Indians," in *Counseling Culturally Different,* ed. Sue, p. 216.

[29] A. Troy, "The Indian in Adolescent Novels," *Indian Historian,* 8 (1975), 32-35.

[30] C. Farris, "The White House Conference on American Indians," *Social Work, 18* (1973), pp. 80-86.

[31] Richardson, "Cultural Perspectives," p. 218.

[32] Richardson, "Cultural Perspectives," p. 218; F. Pepper, "Teaching the American Indian Child in Mainstream Settings," in *Mainstreaming and the Minority Child,* ed. Reginald Jones (Reston, Va.: Council for Exceptional Children, 1976), pp. 133-59.

[33]D. Sue, "Counseling Asian Americans," in *Counseling Culturally Different,* ed. Sue, pp. 113-41.

[34]*Counseling Culturally Different,* ed. Sue.

[35]Gwendolyn Baker, *Multicultural Education: Teaching About Minority Women* (Washington, D.C.: Clearinghouse on Teacher Education, 1977).

[36]*Multicultural Teacher Education* (Washington, D.C.: American Association of Colleges for Teacher Education, 1980).

[37]"Importance of Equal Athletic Opportunity for Women" (Washington, D.C.: Project on Status and Education of Women, 1978).

[38]M. Pines, "Superkids," *Psychology Today,* January 1979, pp. 53-63.

[39]Jesse Jackson, *Push for Excellence* (Chicago, Ill.: Project Excel Headquarters, 1980).

[40]Cheyney, *Teaching Children of Different Cultures in the Classroom* (Columbus, Ohio): Charles Merrill, 1976).

[41]Baker, *Multicultural Education.*

[42]P. Graubard, H. Rosenberg, and M. Martin, "Student Applications of Behavior Modification to Teachers," in *Classroom Management,* Daniel O'Leary, ed. (New York: Pergamon, 1977) pp. 235-49.

[43]Louis Knowles and Kenneth Prewitt, eds., *Institutional Racism in America* (Englewood Cliffs, N.J.: Prentice-Hall, Inc., 1969); Mario Fantini and Gerald Weinstein, *The Disadvantaged: Challenge to Education* (New York: Harper and Row, 1968).

Chapter Eight

[1]Nicholas Colangelo and Ronald Zaffrann, eds. *New Voices in Counseling the Gifted* (Dubuque, Iowa: Kendall/Hunt, 1979).

[2]Colangelo, *New Voices;* Julian Stanley, Danial Keating, and Lynn Fox, *Mathematical Talent* (Baltimore, Md.: John Hopkins University Press, 1974); R. Hogan, "The Gifted Adolescent," in *Handbook of Adolescent Psychology,* ed. Joseph Adelson (New York: John Wiley, 1980), pp. 536-60.

[3]Paul Torrance, *Discovery and Nurturance of Giftedness in the Culturally Different* (Reston, Va.: Council for Exceptional Children, 1977); M. Frazier, "Counseling the Culturally Diverse Gifted," in *Counseling,* ed. Colangelo, pp. 304-11; H. Exum, "Facilitating Psychological and Emotional Development of Gifted Black Students," in *Counseling,* ed. Colangelo, pp. 312-20.

[4]L. Fox, "Sex Differences—Implications for Counseling the Gifted," in *The Gifted and the Creative,* eds. Julian Hanley, William George, and Cecelia Solano (Baltimore, Md.: Johns Hopkins University Press, 1977), pp. 30-42; C. Baruch, "Counseling Girls for the Development of Creativity," in *The Gifted and the Creative,* ed. Hanley, pp. 382-88; P. Casserly, "Helping Able Young Women Take Math and Science Seriously," in *New Voices,* ed. Colangelo, pp, 80-95; P. Wolleat, "Guiding the Career Development of Gifted Females," in *New Voices,* ed. Colangelo, pp. 331-45.

[5]L. Fox and L. Richmond, "Gifted Females: Are We Meeting Their Counseling Needs?" *Personnel and Guidance Journal,* January 1979, pp. 256-61.

[6]L. Sells, "Mathematics, The Critical Filter," *The Science Teacher,* February 1978, pp. 14-21.

[7] Sheila Tobias, *Overcoming Math Anxiety* (New York: W. W. Norton & Co., Inc., 1978); John Ernest, *Math and Sex* (Santa Barbara, Calif.: University of California Math Department, 1976).

[8] James Newell, ed. *Black Mathematicians and Their Works* (New York: William Dorrance & Co., 1980).

[9] Tobias, *Overcoming Math Anxiety.*

[10] S. Tobias, "Anxiety Research in Educational Psychology," *Journal of Educational Psychology,* October 1979, pp. 573-82.

[11] Beeman Phillips, *School, Stress and Anxiety* (New York: N.Y.: Human Sciences, 1978); Charles Spielberger and Irwin Sarason, *Stress and Anxiety* (Washington, D.C.: Hemisphere Press, 1980); R. Hanson, "Anxiety," in *Motivation in Education,* ed., Samuel Ball (New York: Academic Press, 1977), pp. 91-111.

[12] M. Herrick, "The Culturally Disadvantaged and Learning Disabled," *School Psychology Digest,* 5, 1976, pp. 35-40.

[13] J. Throne, "Learning Disabilities: A Radical Behaviorist Point of View," *School Psychology Digest,* 1976, 2, pp. 41-45.

[14] Helen Weiss and Martin Weiss, *A Survival Manual: Case Studies and Suggestions for the L.D. Teenager* (Great Barrington, Mass.: Treehouse Associates, 1974); J. Benjamens, "Learning Disabilities Among Adolescents, *A.P.A. Catalogue of Documents, 7,* 1977, pp. 17-30.

[15] John Carroll and Jeanne Chall, eds. *Toward a Literate Society* (New York: McGraw-Hill, 1975), p. 18.

[16] *Motivational Activities for Reluctant Readers* (Silver Springs, Md.: Project Read, 1979).

[17] *Reading Is Fundamental* (Washington, D.C.: Project R.I.F., 1980).

[18] *Three National Assessments of Reading; 1970-1980* (Denver, Colo.: National Assessment of Education Progress, 1981).

[19] Daniel Fader, *The New Hooked on Books* (New York: Berkeley Publishing, Corp., 1977); Carl Smith and Leo Fay, *Getting People to Read: Volunteer Programs That Work* (New York: Delta Books, 1973).

[20] Frances Maltitz, *Living and Learning in Two Languages* (New York: McGraw-Hill, 1975).

[21] Frank Riddel, ed., *Appalachia: People and Problems* (Dubuque, Iowa: Kendall/Hunt, 1974).

[22] Kathryn Clarenbach, *Educational Needs of Rural Women and Girls* (Washington, D.C.: Women's Education Council, 1977).

[23] Eliot Wigginton, ed., *The Foxfire Book* (New York: Doubleday, 1968), pp. 1-14; Eliot Wigginton, ed., *Foxfire,* vols. 1-4 (New York: Doubleday, 1971, 1973, 1975, 1977).

Chapter Nine

[1] *America's Children and Their Families* (Washington, D.C.: Children's Defense Fund, 1979).

[2] *Children without Homes* (Washington, D.C.: Children's Defense Fund, 1978).

[3] Boston Women's Health Collective, *Our Selves and Our Children* (New York: Random House, 1978).

[4] Lois Hoffman and Ivan Nye, *Working Mothers* (San Francisco, Calif.: Jossey-Bass, 1974).

[5] Daniel Moynihan, *The Negro Family: Case for National Action* (Washington, D.C.: U.S. Department of Labor, 1965).

[6] Robert Staples, *Introduction to Black Sociology* (New York: McGraw-Hill, 1975), pp. 113-50.

[7] Michele Wallace, *Black Macho and the Myth of Superwoman* (New York: Dial Press, 1978); E. Smith, "Cultural and Historical Perspectives in Counseling Blacks," in *Counseling the Culturally Different*, Derald Wing Sue, ed. (New York: Wiley, 1981) pp. 157-61.

[8] Andrew Billingsley, *Black Families in White America* (Englewood Cliffs, N.J.: Prentice-Hall, 1968).

[9] R. Ferrers, *National Longitudinal Study of the High School Class of 1972* (Washington, D.C.: HEW, 1977).

[10] M. Gold and R. Petronio, "Delinquent Behavior in Adolescence," in *Handbook of Adolescent Psychology*, ed. Joseph Adelson (New York: John Wiley, 1980), pp. 495-536.

[11] Staples, *Black Sociology*, pp. 113-50; Joyce Ladner, *Tomorrow's Tomorrow: The Black Woman* (New York: Anchor, 1971).

[12] Marian Edelman, *Portrait of Inequality: Black and White Children in America* (Washington, D.C.: Children's Defense Fund, 1980).

[13] M. Pines, "Superkids," *Psychology Today*, January 1979, pp. 53-63.

[14] Elizabeth Lorton and others, *The Teacher's World* (Washington, D.C.: Clearinghouse for Teacher Education, 1979). M. Floyd, "Schools and Parental Satisfaction," *Phi Delta Kappan*, January 1978, p. 356.

[15] *Children out of School in America* (Washington, D.C.: Children's Defense Fund, 1974).

[16] Herbert Ginsberg, *The Myth of the Deprived Child* (Englewood Cliffs, N.J.: Prentice-Hall, 1972).

[17] R. Bittle, "Improving Parent-Teacher Communication," *Educational Research*, November 1975, pp. 87-95.

[18] J. Jackson, "In Pursuit of Equity, Ethics and Excellence," *Phi Delta Kappan*, November 1978, pp. 191-93.

[19] Thomas Gordon, *Parent Effectiveness Training* (New York: Peter Wyden, 1970); Haim Ginot, *Between Parent and Teenager* (New York: Avon, 1971).

[20] Thomas Gnagney, *How to Put Up with Parents: A Guide for Teenagers* (Ottawa, Ill.: Facilitation House Press, 1975).

[21] Nancy Williamson, *Son or Daughter: Parental Preferences* (Beverly Hills, Calif.: Sage Publications, Inc., 1976).

[22] Barbara Powell, *How to Raise a Successful Daughter* (Chicago: Nelson-Hall Press, 1979); David Lynn, *Daughters and Parents* (Monterey, Calif.: Brooks/Cole, 1979).

[23] James Comer and Alvin Poussant, *Black Child Care* (New York: Simon & Schuster, 1975).

Chapter Ten

[1]Peter Buntman and Eleanor Saris, *How to Live with Your Teenager* (Pasadena, Calif.: Birch Tree Press, 1980), pp. 13-14.

[2]Stanley Coopersmith, *The Myth of the Generation Gap* (Boone, N.C.: Albion Press, 1975); Joseph Adelson, ed., *Handbook of Adolescent Psychology* (New York: Wiley, 1980).

[3]Richard Schmuck and Patricia Schmuck, *Group Processes in the Classroom* (Dubuque, Iowa: Wm. C. Brown, 1979), pp. 194-96; Raymond Adams and Bruce Biddle, *Realities of Teaching: Explorations with Videotape* (New York: Holt, Rinehart & Winston, 1970), p. 89.

[4]Jeremy Brophy and Thomas Good, *Teacher-Student Relationships* (New York: Holt, Rinehart & Winston, 1974), p. 85.

[5]Schmuck, *Processes*, p. 195.

[6]Barry Dollar, *Humanizing Classroom Discipline* (New York: Harper & Row, Pub., 1972), pp. 51-55.

[7]Robert Curwin and Barbara Furhmann, *Discovering Your Teaching Self* (Englewood Cliffs, N.J.: Prentice-Hall, 1975), p. 138.

[8]Irwin Sarason and Barbara Sarason, *Constructive Classroom Behavior* (New York: Human Sciences, 1974).

[9]Alice Gordon, *Games for Growth* (Chicago: Science Research Associates, Inc., 1972); Sam Boocock and Edward Shields, eds., *Simulation Games in Learning* (Beverly Hills, Calif.: Sage Publications, Inc., 1968); William Heitzman, *Educational Games and Simulations* (Washington, D.C.: National Education Association, 1974); R. Slavin, "A Student Team Approach to Teaching Adolescents," *Psychology in the Schools, 14* (1977), pp. 77-84.

[10]P. Twelker, "Some Reflections on Instructional Simulation and Gaming," *Simulations and Games,* June 1972, pp. 147-53; G. Gaines, "Toward a More Systematic Evaluation of Classroom Simulations and Games," *Simulations and Games,* July 1973, p. 241.

[11]Alan Gartner, *Children Teach Children* (New York: Harper & Row, Pub., 1971).

[12]*Youth Counsels Youth* (New York: National Commission on Resources for Youth, 1978).

[13]"High School Tracking," *Inequality in Education,* July 1972, pp. 18-19; David and Robert Johnson, *Learning Together and Alone* (Englewood Cliffs, N.J.: Prentice-Hall, 1975); J. Comer, "The Circle Game in School Tracking," *Inequality in Education,* July 1972, pp. 23-26; Thomas Good and Jeremy Brophy, *Looking in Classrooms* (New York: Harper & Row, 1978).

[14]Reginald Jones, ed., *Mainstreaming and the Minority Child* (Reston, Va.: Council for Exceptional Children, 1976); Marian Edelman, *Portrait of Inequality* (Washington, D.C.: Children's Defense Fund, 1980), pp. 74-75.

[15]Michael Rutter and others, *15,000 Hours* (Cambridge, Mass.: Harvard University Press, 1979), p. 13.

[16]*Ability Grouping: Research Summary* (Washington, D.C.: National Education Association, 1968).

Chapter Eleven

[1] R. Winett and R. Winkler, "Be Still, Be Quiet, Be Docile," *Applied Behavior Analysis, 5* (1972), pp. 499-504.

[2] Bernard Skinner, *The Technology of Teaching* (New York: Appleton-Century-Crofts, 1968).

[3] Robert Williams and James Long, *Toward a Self Managed Lifestyle* (Boston: Houghton Mifflin, 1977); Dwight Goodwin and Thomas Coates, *Helping Students Help Themselves* (Englewood Cliffs, N.J.: Prentice-Hall, 1976); Michael Mahoney and Carl Thoresen, eds., *Self Control: Power to the Person* (Monterey, Calif.: Brooks/Cole, 1974); Arnold Goldstein, Robert Sprafkin, and Jane Gershaw, *I Know What's Wrong But I Don't Know What to Do About It* (Englewood Cliffs, N.J.: Prentice-Hall, 1979); Marvin Goldfried and Michael Merbaum, eds., *Behavior Change Through Self Control* (New York: Holt, Rinehart & Winston, 1973).

[4] Deane Shapiro, *Precision Nirvana* (Englewood Cliffs, N.J.: Prentice-Hall, 1978); Don Hamachek, *Encounters with the Self* (New York: Holt, Rinehart & Winston, 1978).

[5] Carl Riggs, ed., *Bibliotherapy* (Newark, Del.: International Reading Association, 1971).

[6] *The Bookfinder* (Circle Pines, Minn.: American Guidance, 1977).

[7] *The New Model Me* (Lakewood, Ohio: Board of Education, 1973).

[8] Rian McMullen and Bill Casey, *Talk Sense to Yourself* (Golden, Colo.: Counseling Research Institute, 1975); Charles Zastrow, *Talk to Yourself: Using the Power of Self Talk* (Englewood Cliffs, N.J.: Prentice-Hall, 1979).

[9] Robert Alberti and Michael Emmons, *Your Perfect Right: A Guide to Assertive Behavior* (San Luis Obispo, Calif.: Impact Press, 1974); Robert Bolton, *People Skills: How to Assert Yourself* (Englewood Cliffs, N.J.: Prentice-Hall, 1977).

[10] J. Galassi and M. Galassi, "Self Expression Scale," *Behavior Therapy, 5* (1974), pp. 165-71.

[11] John Kackley, *Helping Students Survive at Home and at School* (Gainesville, Fla.: University of Florida, 1975); P. Graubard, H. Rosenberg, and M. Martin, "Student Applications of Behavior Modification to Teachers," in *Classroom Management*, eds. Daniel O'Leary and Susan O'Leary (Elmsford, N.Y.: Pergamon Press, 1977), pp. 235-49.

[12] Neil Postman and Charles Weingartner, *The Soft Revolution* (New York: Delacorte Press, 1971).

[13] Thomas Szaz, *Heresies* (Garden City, N.Y.: Anchor Press, 1976), p. 15.

Index